Super Skills for Supervisors

A Narrative Approach to Developing Supervisory Skills

By

Frank Buchar

authorHOUSE™

1663 LIBERTY DRIVE, SUITE 200
BLOOMINGTON, INDIANA 47403
(800) 839-8640
WWW.AUTHORHOUSE.COM

First published by AuthorHouse 01/22/05

ISBN: 1-4208-1163-0 (e)
ISBN: 1-4208-1161-4 (sc)

Printed in the United States of America
Bloomington, Indiana

This book is printed on acid-free paper.

Table of Contents

Super Skill: Improve Work Processes

Dedication

This book is dedicated to the Inuit, past, present, and future, for their creation and ongoing development of the arctic stone figures known generally as inukshuks.

In this book, the inukshuk is used as symbol for giving direction, supervisory direction.

Acknowledgments

A special note of thanks to Rick Bolek of Bolek & Associates, for suggesting the idea for this book and for planting the seed.

I would also like to thank Mick Ellis of the Ottawa-based MTE Group for the many conversations we shared together on supervisory and management issues.

To my son, Marco, thank you for the graphic illustrations of the inukshuks presented in **Super Skills for Supervisors**.

Cover design by artist Ward Shipman.

Foreword: Super Skills for Supervisors

In this book you'll enjoy listening to conversations between and among five front line supervisors- people in different lines of work with different problems, from both the private and public sectors. It's about how they get together to enjoy dim sum at a Chinese restaurant every other Thursday to discuss their common problems in supervision. It's a time and a place where they can vent their feelings and think of ways to help each other out. Five supervisors who also happen to be friends and who like each other's company. Together they sort through all of the problems that make up the daily grind of a front line supervisor.

But before we meet them and get to know their situations, let's take a look at the front line supervisory role itself. What makes it special? What are the parts about the role that aren't so good? How does it change a person? The best way to start is to listen to one of the supervisors that we'll meet in these pages, someone typical enough to draw some conclusions from:

"Front line supervisors are treated like dirt at my plant. Worse than dirt- they're treated like grunge under your refrigerator. We don't get respect. I don't want to sound like some fanatic about the respect thing, but it's the truth, so help

me. We're not included. We're out of the loop. Sometimes I'm the last to hear about things. Communication... yeah that's a laugh. A sticky note on my computer screen when I start a shift - that's about as far as it goes. And oh yeah, I do the dirty work when it comes around to it. I get it from both sides."

Just a thread of a conversation, but if we've listened well, we can pick up on a few things. What's really striking, and this is widespread across the supervisory spectrum, is the feeling that human dignity has been lost somehow, or suspended, or at least allowed to lapse. The Supervisor doesn't feel respected in his or her role. That's the first issue. Then we move right into the team issue of not being included: " Am I in, or am I out?" The answer is a resounding "no." Communication is a joke, a post-it note with some instruction to do something. The last comment is about "dirty work," signaling the kind of tough disciplinary situations that a front line supervisor often faces. It's about being caught in the middle between management and subordinate staff.

These are some of the themes we'll be exploring together in this book. It fills a great need. The training that's provided here in these pages is meant to be accessible, and even enjoyable, like reading short stories or dialogues from a play. They're meant to be shared and talked about. That's why I've created stories around these front line supervisors. I wanted to make supervisory concepts and approaches come alive. I've done this in order to illustrate some very practical ideas. The Supervisors in these pages are based on real life characters, people who work in settings not too different from your own. We'll use these imaginary Supervisors to "flesh out" useful ideas on front line supervision.

The ideas on supervision presented in these pages are not new, just as common sense is not new. The intention is to present these common sense ideas in a fresh, and accessible way, through dialogue. The front line supervisors depicted here discuss these ideas on supervisory management and share their insights freely, using them as a basis for action in their different workplaces. Through their conversations, and the scenarios that they encounter in their common role, the "Supers" define and hone their skills, despite the difficulties inherent in their position. Each of the chapters begins with the title of the supervisory skill presented and a brief profile of the Super involved. All of the chapters are followed by the graphic representation of an inukshuk defining the skill set presented. The inukshuk drawing is there to serve as a useful summary or memory aid for the supervisory skill explored.

Front line supervisors are on the fault line between management and employees, pressured equally by both groups, and expected to perform miracles with little incentive- usually for only a ten to fifteen per cent uplift in salary. In most cases, they receive precious little training to equip them for the supervisory role. That's the reason behind this book: front line supervisors need simple and yet elegant solutions to their common, ongoing problems.

Introduction: Of Dim Sum, Inukshuks, and Supervision

"What can I get you sir?"

"You know something," Terry said, as he studied the menu, "I'll wait a bit on that until my friends arrive." Terry peered over the top of his glasses and saw a young girl with a slim build and a dimpled smile that could melt an iceberg. She poured him some tea. Behind her, an older woman was pushing a cart loaded with a dozen, small, steaming bamboo-baskets. The aroma was delightful.

Terry enjoyed the lightness and informality of the lunches. He was surprised at how inexpensive the delicacies were. Raymond had told him that Dim Sums were a Cantonese specialty consisting mostly of meat or sea-food stuffings wrapped in thin dough skin. He had said that the term "dim sum" meant "treasures of the heart," and he was beginning to understand why. Since their first Dim Sum luncheon meetings, Terry had grown fond of the variety of miniature dishes that were served. There were wonderful steamed buns stuffed with roast pork or savory chicken and small chopped spare-ribs or pieces of chicken wrapped in bean-curd skin. He remembered his surprise at how tasty chicken claws could be. He had never even thought of chicken claws as edible before now. Before Raymond had introduced him and the other Supervisors to the Cantonese restaurant, he had only thought of Chinese food as fried rice dishes with sweet and sour pork ribs and breaded chicken balls. Terry smiled at his adaptability to authentic Chinese food.

Terry looked at his watch: twenty-to-twelve. He was early. He smiled at the girl. She seemed to enjoy her work. He looked around. It was just beginning to get busy.

Terry loved these Thursday luncheons held every other week. In a few minutes the group would be here and the fun could begin. He wondered how the luncheon meetings had all started. All of them were front line supervisors. All of them lived in the city. But they were from different work environments. Not one of them was in the same business. Maybe that's what made the discussions so interesting. They applied the same general supervisory skills in altogether different settings in both the public and private sectors. He knew what he wanted to talk about tonight. Maybe, he thought, that's why he was here so early. He wanted some feedback from people he respected. Each time they met they focused on one topic that they could talk about informally and easily.

He settled back into the chair and thought about his problem at the plant. Training. It was all about training, and he didn't know where to start. The thought of it took him away from the comfortable Chinese restaurant where he was sitting and he was suddenly back on the plant floor. In his mind's eye he saw the million dollar computerized machines at the engine plant. Huge machines that the vendors had only recently installed. The vendors had spent most of their time with the engineers, and there hadn't been any time for the training that was promised. His tool-setters needed training to operate the new equipment. Terry had deadlines to meet. He knew that he couldn't even start until the tool-setters were trained.

"Hey Terry... space control to Major Tom... you look a million miles away. How are you doing?"

Terry looked up to see Marty Hessler, the muscular police corporal with a grin as big as Alberta, the province where he was originally from. He was dressed casually in jeans and a dark blue sweatshirt.

" Good to see you," Terry said. "Geez, I was so deep in thought I didn't see you come in."

"So, what's up? What made you look so intense when I first came in?"

"Well, I've got tons of new equipment on the floor that no one knows how to run. I've got a start production date in a few weeks with management breathing down my neck. I've also got a bunch of people sitting idle for most of the day. So yeah, that's why I'm looking a bit intense."

"Hmm, not so good," Marty said softly.

"What about you. Things going O.K.?"

Marty shook his head. "Back at the detachment we're just about to get into a big change initiative, a new software system, and they're not going to like it. Seems that Headquarters gets a brainstorm every once in a while, and then we have to live with it. I haven't even seen the new system yet, but they're telling me to make sure everything runs smoothly."

"Change," Terry said. "That's the word these days, but you know what they say… 'the only person who likes change is a baby with a wet diaper.' "

Marty laughed, waving over to a threesome just entering.

"I've got a feeling it's going to be an interesting lunch. Here they come," Marty said, extending his arm and motioning to the three remaining members of the group to join them. The restaurant was filling fast with only one small table beside their own that was still free.

They greeted one another warmly and then settled into their chairs. The newcomers included Gary Clark, Sylvie Morriseau, and Raymond Tang. They glanced at the menus, but already knew what they wanted. Only rarely did they order an item from the menu. The group of them ordered from the dim sum cart as it stopped by each table.

Each of them selected their choice to share with the group, and then, round robin fashion, as always, they asked each other what was the "hot button" since their last meeting, two weeks earlier. The "hot button" was any issue or problem or situation that they were faced with as Supervisors.

Terry and Marty went over what they had already talked about, and then it was Gary's turn. Gary was the newest Super on the block. Jokingly, among themselves, they referred to each other as "Supers." Gary was dubbed a "Super" when he had made a wonderful rant a few weeks before, just a few days after being promoted to Supervisor.

"Front line supervisors are treated like dirt at my plant. Worse than dirt- they're treated like grunge under your refrigerator. We don't get respect. I don't want to sound like some fanatic about the respect thing, but it's the truth, so help me. We're not included. We're out of the loop. Sometimes I'm the last to hear about things. Communication… yeah that's a laugh. A sticky note on my computer screen when I start a shift - that's about as far as it goes. And oh yeah, I do the dirty work when it comes around to it. I get it from both sides. I just wish someone would tell me what they expect me to do. Is that so much to ask?"

They had clapped and cheered when Gary had his rant, because each of them knew what he meant. Each of them had experienced it first-hand. That was still Gary's hot button: what do you expect a Supervisor to do?

For Sylvie, the issue was on how work was done, on the processes involved in getting work done. She carefully observed the way a product moved down the line, the many little changes that happened to it before the cycle of production was finished. She was keen on making things better, on continuous improvement. Sylvie was a strong believer in teamwork and on how that affected work processes. But what she was finding was that team issues held her back from making the production gains she wanted. The soft side of the operation, the people side, was the part that was stopping her from moving ahead. It frustrated her and made her angry because she thought it was just obstinate, stubborn people that were proving to be the problem.

Raymond Tang's hot button was problem solving. He wanted to know all about the practical tools he could use to solve problems and to come up with good solutions. He felt that facilitative approaches to problems could make all the difference in the world. Raymond was committed to making sure that he had the best tools for problem solving right there at his fingertips. He was thinking about that as he savored his first chicken wing. It was perfect.

"These wings are fantastic. You know," Raymond said, " if I could make a product that would make my customer as happy as I am with this wing right now, life would be perfect."

"Well, I'll bet you any money it's in the way it's made, the process," Sylvie said.

"You might think so," Terry interrupted, "but I think it's also a question of training. Training is where we have to focus too. That's the linchpin that drives things. I can say that because I'm living with the lack of it right now where I work. I've got million dollar machines standing idle because no one knows how to operate them. The people who sold us the machines have left because we couldn't train them in the few days the vendor trainers were at the plant."

"I beg to differ," Sylvie said. "Sure, the training is important at the start, when you've got to get people familiar with basic start and stop functions, but that's not the real problem. I mean, we have to look at the way a work operation affects the floor, the process or system involved."

"Yes, but everyone has to know their role, and what's expected of them," Gary interjected loudly, his voice rising. "Before the training, before all the steps involved in getting something done, you have to know the expectations behind it all. I'm still not sure of what they want me to do."

"Hey, I can hear you Gary. Keep it down a bit. We don't want to cause a public disturbance," Marty said. "Heck, what about me? I've got a big change to prepare my people for, and no clear direction on the impact of the change, and how it's going to change everything they've done before."

"Well folks, looks like we've all got some hot buttons," Terry said. "I know I wanted to discuss my training problem, but ever since Gary's famous rant a few weeks back, I think we need to give his issue an airing first. What do you say? Let's start with the expectations a Supervisor needs to do his job. All agreed?"

Everyone nodded, looking to Gary to start things off. "Thanks. I appreciate that. I can't tell you how tough it's been these last few weeks. I mean I've been wondering if I'm cut out to be a Super. I sure had fewer hassles when I was on the floor along with everybody else. Maybe you can give me a few suggestions. Hey Raymond, what is it that you're doodling on that napkin"?

"It's a drawing of a stone figure built by the Inuit in the high arctic. It's called an inukshuk. They were used for many purposes. Sometimes they gave direction to travelers. Sometimes they pointed out where game could be found. They're said to be objects that act in the capacity of a human being. I like the simplicity of the symbol, and its elegance. I use them to capture ideas sometimes, like mind maps. Don't worry. I've been listening carefully. I think we can talk about a lot of supervisory issues, and your situation is the best place to begin."

Super Skill: Clarify Expectations

Profile One: Gary Clark

Gary Clark has been a front line supervisor at SmarTech Industries, a manufacturer of novelty items, for three months. He is new to the supervisory role and does not have an electronics background. He spent his first two weeks on the job with a Supervisor who was retiring from SmarTech, a man who wasn't really interested in sharing his knowledge. Gary did not receive any formal training in supervisory skills or in basic electronics. He is trying hard to convince the assembly line staff that the new computerized machinery recently installed and operating will streamline work flow enabling them to produce 30% more items. He is telling them what SmarTech management has told him to tell them. Many of the line staff are resistant to changes that will affect them. One person in particular is trying to use Gary's lack of supervisory experience against him. Neither he nor any of his staff has been included in any significant communication about the new equipment. Gary has also been excluded from the decision-making process. What bothers him most is that no one in management has told him what he's expected to do. He is trying to do a good job, but his quandary is to define his role in the absence of any meaningful management direction. Through his luncheon meetings with the other Supervisors, Gary begins to define and profile essential supervisory skills.

At the Plant

Long after his shift was over, Gary sat in his tiny office feeling overwhelmed by his new responsibilities. He felt frantically lost. He couldn't seem to get a handle on what he was supposed to do. He gazed up at the whiteboard on the wall. It was completely blank, much like the way he felt. In front of him, on his metal desk, was the job description for the supervisory position he had applied for. Full of the kind of general, abstract words that looked good on paper, but didn't mean a thing on the plant floor. It was like a map that didn't fit the territory. How was he going to translate that vague description of his new job into something that he could sink his teeth into. He brushed back his mop of thick brown hair with the back of his hand the way he always did when he was at a loss for what to do.

A large figure walked past the large office window to his right. It was Jim Ferris, the plant manager, one of the managers who had hired him. Gary quickly left his office and called out to Jim who was doing his rounds on the plant floor. Jim turned abruptly and offered the briefest of smiles before his face settled back into the grim, lined features that were most familiar to everyone.

"Jim, you got a minute?"

"Yeah, I got one Gary."

They went into Gary's office, where Gary sat down while Jim remained standing though there was another chair next to Gary's.

"Can you go over this job description with me? I want to make sure I get everything right."

Jim sighed, looking perplexed. "Look, I've got a dozen things I have to do. Can it wait? Besides, didn't we go over everything during the interview? Is it a human resources thing?"

"No, no, I'm fine with my contract. I just want to make sure I'm doing what you want me to do."

"Look, all it boils down to is a 30% increase in our production. That's what we want. Just that, and nothing more. I'm busy now. Can we do it some other time?" Jim was standing in front of him, disappointment clearly etched across his face.

"It won't take long. I just need some clear direction on this," Gary said awkwardly, turning the job description sideways for Jim to see it better.

"Look, do I need to tell you what to do? That's why we hired you. I've got to run. You'll catch on. Just concentrate on getting that 30% increase. Bye."

Gary felt even more terrible than before. He shoved the job description into a folder and slammed it roughly into the metal file cabinet. He brushed back his hair with a sharp flick of his wrist and decided to go home. On the drive home, he began to wonder if he could get his old job back. He was good in sales, even though he didn't like being on the road. Anything was better than this, feeling altogether useless and out of it. At least in sales he had his self-respect, something more than he was getting at SmarTech. The old buzzard who was supposed to show him the ropes left him without a clue. He stopped on the way home for a workout at his fitness club, and by the time he opened his front door he felt human again. Tomorrow was another day.

Gary knew that he had to convince his assembly line people that the new configuration on the line was going to work. The trouble was that he wasn't sure whether it was going to or not. His knowledge of electronics was limited to programming his VCR and downloading music from the internet. Beyond that, he was in unknown territory. He walked along the line and observed his staff monitoring their machine controls. He needed to get a handle on what was going on. Tommy Johnson gave him a big toothy grin.

"Hi Tommy, everything O.K.?"

"So far, so good. But that 30% production increase is a pipe-dream."

"Why do you say that?"

"The machine keeps seizing up. There's way too much downtime. I think they bought a lemon." Tommy was a stocky, little man with a bored expression on his face that never seemed to leave.

"Can we do anything to stop the downtime?" Gary asked.

"If the engineers can't figure it out, I sure can't. Remember I just work here. They never ask my opinion anyway. By the way Gary, I'd like to take a few days off next week to do some fishing. I've got some overtime built up, and I'd like to use that. What do you think buddy?"

A machine operator working at a similar machine was listening intently to their conversation. Gary's back was turned to him.

"I didn't know about the overtime. I haven't checked the overtime log. Is that kept in the Supervisor's office?"

"Well yeah, but I haven't had a chance yet to do the paperwork for this last bit of time I put in."

"Who authorized it?"

"Well, no one, but unless I had stayed, the machine wouldn't have operated."

"Who was the Supervisor on that night?"

"That guy who retired, Murphy."

"Well, I guess it's O.K. Make sure you get that form to me."

"Sure thing Gary. I'll bring you back some nice walleye."

Tommy winked at the machine operator across from him when Gary turned to leave. Tommy smirked behind Gary's back and then checked his calendar.

On the way back to his office, Gary passed the first work station on the line, the responsibility of Vinko Grubisic, an experienced machine operator. Vinko was adept at solving any problems that stopped production. He seemed to enjoy meeting technical challenges head on. It was as if the problems he encountered were an opponent's chess moves. He tinkered with things until they flowed easily. Vinko was very soft-spoken, almost shy. He rarely took credit for solving any problems that came up. He simply said that if you watched closely how things moved on the line you could easily find out where the problem was.

"Vinko, is the new machinery working out O.K.?"

"Yes Gary, it is. Some changes from before, but they're working out. It will take a little time though, to figure out how the machine works. The engineer was showing me what to look out for on the computer screen, and I'm beginning to understand it." As Vinko spoke, Gary noticed that he held a well-used and battered multi-purpose tool that had seen better days.

"I sure wish I could get the big picture. It's all so new to me that it's going to take a little time to see how everything is working together," Gary said surveying Vinko's workstation. Vinko kept everything in his work area incredibly clean even though a maintenance crew looked after basic clean up.

"Just watch and listen to the machines. That's what I do. Look at what goes in, and look at what comes out. That's the best way to figure it all out," Vinko said, pointing to an item on the screen. See." Gary noticed the delight in Vinko's eyes when he said this.

"Yeah, I think I know what you mean."

"It's all very confusing at first, especially for someone new. It was hard for me to understand the operation at first. I wish Jim Ferris had asked me what was good about the old operation, before they installed the new machinery. It had some good features too, but that's how it goes around here. If you like, I'll explain this part of the operation to you, and you can follow it along down the line."

"I'd like that very much Vinko."

Then, for about twenty minutes Vinko showed Gary the basic machine operation, and how it interfaced with the second machine on the line. Vinko explained things very slowly and carefully, simplifying what was taking place so that Gary could understand the process. He suggested that Gary follow the line through to the end and get a sense of how things worked. Gary listened to Vinko's kind, thoughtful summary of the machine's operation, and then he asked a few questions that Vinko thought were astute. By the time he left the workstation, he was feeling elated. The sounds of the workplace, people tending their machines and equipment, invigorated him and signaled a challenge and an opportunity for him that he had not experienced before.

Over the next days Gary studied work reports and production sheets that were finally beginning to make sense. He worked hard to understand what the data meant, and his new understanding impelled him to find ways to make solid improvements that could translate into real production goals. He was just beginning to feel confident about these first steps when Jim Ferris stormed into his office. He was fuming. Ferris was a large, balding man with an expression on his lined face that usually appeared to be vexed. His face looked ready to explode with large veins bulging at his temples.

"Gary, what's this about Johnson's overtime. I didn't sign any authorization for him to take a few days overtime leave."

"Tommy submitted an overtime sheet to me and I signed it," Gary said, more than a little shocked at Jim's threatening presence.

"I'm the only one who can authorize that. Now we're going to have more downtime than we've had before. Who told you that you could do that?"

"Well I just assumed I could."

"Assumed! Look, Johnson's a guy you've got to watch. He'll take any chance he can to slack off. Didn't Murphy tell you about him?"

"No. Murphy was the Supervisor on duty the times that Johnson worked overtime."

"Murphy didn't sign the form. You did."

"I don't know what to say Jim. I only signed it because I thought I could."

"You thought you could. That's some reason. Like I said, I'm the only one who can authorize it. Got it?"

"I do now," Gary said, flicking a lock of his hair back nervously.

"Get with the program. Make sure Vinko takes over Johnson's machine, and get Peters to look after Work Station One."

Jim shook his head in disgust and left as abruptly as he had entered. Gary was stunned. He pounded his fist on the desk in sheer exasperation. How was he supposed to know the correct procedures when no one had told him about them in the first place? Here we go again, he thought to himself in silent anger. He wondered if he should call up his old boss to find out if his former sales position had been filled. He didn't want to make the call. Working at SmarTech was allowing him to spend far more time with Carly, his six-year-old daughter, than he had ever had before. He didn't want to go on the road again. He wanted to stay at SmarTech, but he didn't know if he could take what was coming his way.

Thursday Dim Sum

Gary had hardly sipped his tea. He looked around at the others after he had finished telling his story. He wondered if any of them had ever gone through what he was going through. He sighed, smoothing back a hank of hair that had fallen across his forehead. "What do you think? Any suggestions?" The Supervisors glanced at each other quickly, looking to see who wanted to begin.

"Gary, I hear what you're saying. Some of the details might be a little different, but I've been there," Terry said. "I know it might be a hard thing to do given the way you've described the manager, but you've got to sit down with him and get the lay of the land."

"What do you mean?" Gary said.

"Find out in clear terms what's expected of you. That's the first step. Get him to define your role as a Supervisor. Without that you're just going to be spinning your wheels. He's got to give you scope. You've said that he wants that 30% production increase and that's a good target, something to aim for, but it's not nearly enough. "

7

"Yeah, you've got to do that," Sylvie said, using her hands to emphasize the point as she always did. "Sit down with the guy and ask him point blank what he expects you to do. Ask him to meet with you on a regular basis. It sounds like he's on the plant floor quite a bit. Maybe he's even doing some of your job."

Marty had listened thoughtfully to what had been said. He knew what it was like to begin a new job without clear direction.

"You're right on about the job description," Marty said. "Sure doesn't help much. Meeting with him and listening is what has to be done. I mean really listening. Make sure you take notes. It could be that the manager isn't too clear himself on what a Supervisor does. But that's an opportunity too. Together you can really map out the coordinates of what you have to do."

"I think you're being a little too hard on job descriptions," Raymond said. "If a job description is well written, it can be a key tool in generating expectations. A starting point at least. For instance, Gary told us about the overtime sheet and work reports he was studying. Those records are a supervisor's tools. That to me means that record keeping is an important part of his role. He needs those tools and the data they provide to reach the 30% production increase his manager wants. Besides, Gary's staff will probably have job descriptions for their jobs as well. If Gary reviews their job profiles, he can get a good head start on knowing what they're expected to do, and that kind of job knowledge can help him determine what training or coaching they need. He needs to know what's expected of them as well. What I'm saying is that in order to get the clear expectations he wants for his job, he has to prepare and take the initiative to get at some basic information. Does that make sense Gary?"

"Yeah, it does. I've been looking at records, like you mentioned, but I hadn't thought about using job descriptions in that way."

Terry finished eating a steamed pork ball and wiped his hands with a napkin. In just a few minutes he had devoured five of them. He licked his lips with satisfaction. "From what Gary's said about the guy who took overtime, I think he may have a discipline problem on his hands sooner or later. I've had a problem child or two in my time, and that's a big part of our job, keeping control I mean, and looking after discipline. Things can get out of control if you let things slide."

"Sure is a major part of my job," Marty said, sipping at his tea. When I first got my stripes, I didn't know whether or not to be a buddy or a boss. I learned the hard way that the old 'command and control' style is not so good when you want staff to be part of a team. Times when I was the buddy, it backfired when I had to be the boss. It's a fine line, the control issue. I mean you want to keep your people happy and motivated, but people are people, and sometimes you run into people who don't want to play by the rules, and I'm not talking about the bad guys. I'm talking about fellow police officers."

"Right on," Terry said, picking up a spring roll and dipping it in soya sauce.

"I found that the situation you're faced with determines the kind of supervision that is best. Sometimes you have to lay down the law. Some people will test you to see what they can get away with. If you try to be a buddy with a certain type of person, they see it as a weakness they can exploit. Not a nice thing, but it happens."

Well," Gary said, "that's exactly what happened to me lately, and I sure didn't like it."

"The other thing, and it's bugging me right now, " Terry continued, " is training. I really need to get my people trained on new machinery, but that's a subject for another time. You know, it's a funny thing. So many of us become supervisors without getting any training in the people skills, the soft skills. All the focus it seems is on the technical side. That's very important, but what I see in your situation is the need for training in supervision. Sure, you need to get your expectations nailed down, but you also need to get some useful ideas under your belt on how to deal with people. How do you get them to cooperate with you? How do you motivate them? How do you discipline people when you have to? How do you create schedules and shifts that people are happy with? It takes years to develop a skilled electrician, and that means a lot of training. But what about the time needed to develop a supervisor? The new supervisor is lost in the shuffle. I don't know of any 'natural' supervisors. It takes training to cut down the learning curve. What do you think Raymond? You've had the most experience as a Super."

Raymond was thin and wiry, with wispy strands of graying hair and sharp, assessing eyes.

Raymond smiled, "I sure wish I'd gotten some supervisory training at the beginning. It could have saved me a lot of time and a lot of grief. For instance, take the issue of discipline. When I fist came across people problems, I thought the Human Resources Department handled that. So I sent them to HR, but that took up a lot of my time. I had to explain what happened, and things just took so long. It took me a long time to realize that part of my job was to deal with it, and deal with it early. Later, I only involved HR when I needed to, and not before."

Raymond noticed an anxious look on Gary's face. "Gary, you look like there's something wrong. "You don't agree?"

"No," Gary replied. "It's just that all of you are saying a lot of good things. I'll never remember it all, and I want to."

"Tell you what," Raymond said, "I'll be the scribe. "I'll take notes on what we talk about. I'll use an inukshuk drawing or what's called an 'imitation person' to capture the main points. Is that O.K.?" Everyone nodded. "I'll make sure everybody gets a copy."

Gary's face relaxed. "I sure would appreciate that Raymond."

"All of us would," Sylvie said.

"Only trouble is," Raymond said, "If I'm recording the key points that come up in our discussions, you may not always agree with what I put down."

10

"You know," Marty said, "that's where one of my skills as an investigator comes in. I've had to learn to listen very closely to what people say to get things right. I'm still learning about listening. I can help out there, if you want to fax me a drawing first to check out if I heard the same things you did."

"I like that," Raymond replied. "Though we may not always agree on what the key points were."

""You're right there," Marty said. " What a person hears is usually what they're predisposed to hear. But that's a good thing. We can use any problems we have on that score to get at communication skills. I've been thinking about that a lot lately. I've always thought that Supers have to spend a lot of their time in communicating."

"So," Raymond said, "let's do a quick summary so far of what we've covered. Today, we're focusing on expectations, on how important it is for a new Supervisor to get clear expectations from management. Am I right? So, in order to do that, Gary has to take the initiative and prepare for the meeting with his manager. That means collecting all the necessary data, and reviewing a lot of job descriptions, including his own."

Terry raised a half-eaten barbequed pork bun and said, "I'd say that clear expectations are important for a Supervisor at any stage of his career. If you don't get crystal clear expectations, you'll never be able to do your job well. You'll always be second guessing management, trying to fill in blanks that you should have filled in together with management." Terry emphasized his point with a flourish of his pork bun and ended it with a final pass into his mouth.

"O.K. then," Sylvie said, "the first thing is being prepared for the meeting with your manager. You have to review your job description, of course, but you also have to have a good understanding of what your staff does, each of them. I sure agree with you on that point Raymond. You have to know their jobs in detail. Gary, you've already said you reviewed work reports and production information. That's a good start. But you have to get on the floor and watch things, observe the way people are working. You need to get familiar with the workflow, especially with the new machines. I'm talking about the need-to-know stuff. The nice-to-know stuff can come later. Raymond, do you agree?"

"Sure do," Raymond nodded, jotting down his notes on an unused napkin. "Sylvie, I think what you've been saying, if I can summarize your points in my own words, is that you have to optimize teams. Your second point, about observing the workflow, is all about improving work processes. Is that summary O.K, with you?"

"Yes, that's it exactly, Sylvie answered. " Optimizing teams and improving work processes."

"Now it's my turn," Marty said, putting his tea-cup down on the white, plastic covered table. " You've got to talk with your people. Listen to what they have to say. Find out what their problems are. You've got to identify their concerns with the new equipment. The important thing is to ask the right kinds of questions to draw them out. Ask the big questions, sure, but don't forget to ask the little questions too. Like they say, the devil is in the details. Do they need training on the new equipment? Do they have the basic skills they need to ensure training will be effective? You've got to manage change. It's pretty darned hard to operate a spanking new computerized machine when you don't have basic computer skills. Investigate the situation and then once you've listened to them, make sure you repeat to them what they've said, only in your own words, to make sure you got it right. It's all about good communication. Good listening is the first step, but it takes practice."

Marty glanced around the table looking for any non-verbal cues that might signal disagreement. He'd often discovered that a quick, observant glance at the people around him spoke volumes about any misunderstandings or confusion that might arise over what he had said. Everyone around the table appeared to be in agreement.

Sylvie leaned forward on her elbows, mirroring Marty's posture. "Marty, what techniques do you use to listen well?"

"Well, I try to get the general drift of what's being said first off. Then I listen for details. I separate the facts from the feelings. Think of it like that old painting on the wall there, the one with fishermen in the foreground. The background there, the distant horizon and the sea set the general mood, the overall feeling. That foreground is like the details you want to take note of. It takes a bit of practice at first, but it's worth the effort. Sometimes there are blocks or barriers to listening. A person may feel that nothing will be done with the information they offer, or they may bring up other work-related issues that have nothing to do with what you're asking them. Another potential listening problem is the difference between the speed of thinking and listening, something I picked up at a training workshop. Pretty easy for this differential to become a problem, a listening block, when you consider that we can listen and think at about three times the rate that we can speak. Most people listen superficially. They're using the extra thinking time they have to plan what they're going to say next rather than listening attentively. It's really hard work to listen well. Once I think I've understood what's being said, what the basic facts are, and what feelings or opinions surround those facts, I summarize it in my mind. Then, I let the person know what I heard, and I ask if my interpretation is correct. Mind you, I don't say word for word what the person speaking said. I just try to get some common understanding to begin with. And keep in mind that the questions you ask are very, very important. You can start with an open-ended question, such as, 'What do you think about the new equipment on the floor?' You can follow that with a closed type of question, the kind of question where you want a basic yes or no, such as 'Do you need any extra training on this machine?'"

"Gotcha," Raymond said, looking up at Marty. "The key skill is 'Communicate: listen, then present.' Oh yes, and you've also got to manage change. I think you mentioned that earlier, right?"

"You've got it," Marty said.

Gary looked across the table at Raymond. Raymond was drawing lines that looked like a stone figure in the middle of his napkin. Around the figure were smaller doodles, circles with lines radiating from them. "Hey Raymond, what are you scribbling?"

Raymond chuckled, his eyes shining. " Believe it or not, I'm taking notes. It's an offshoot of mind-mapping. I use it to focus my thinking," he said holding up the napkin for everyone to see.

"There. What do you think of my supervisory inukshuk?"

"What's an inukshuk again? It looks like some kind of stone figure."

"An inukshuk is an Inuit word. It means 'imitation person.' It's an icon from the high north, the arctic. It gives meaning on a number of different levels. People traveling across the Canadian arctic expanses would build one pointing out the way for others to follow. Can you imagine the feeling a lone traveler would feel when seeing one? A rough likeness of a human being cast together from a bunch of loose rocks. Inukshuks give direction. That's why I've used it as a symbol for us to follow, a supervisory inukshuk. It'll make it easier for us to remember all of the skills or competencies involved. Each stone is a competency. We can even add to the overall structure if we like."

"It's a great idea. I like the way you say that the inukshuk gives direction. That's what I need."

"That's what we all need."

"At the top of my drawing, I've printed 'Clarify Expectations,' to zero in on the discussion. It's in Cantonese so you won't be able to make it out until I've put it into English on the graphic I give you at our next meeting. I've added some more stones to represent some of the other ideas we've discussed. I picked up the technique years ago at a workshop on brainstorming techniques. It was all about problem solving and used ideas from people like Edward de Bono and Tony Buzan."

"Funny isn't it," Sylvie said, "I mean how what a supervisor needs to know touches on so many different areas. Getting clear expectations depends on preparing yourself and communicating in the right way. It's all related. It's all connected."

"Yeah," Gary said, "I feel better already. I really appreciate this. Raymond, I sure hope I can decipher those notes of yours."

"Don't worry. What I'll give you, once I've cleaned it up, will be simple and clear. A one-page graphic summary, an inukshuk. Nothing unnecessary, just the need-to-know stuff. I'm going to run it by Marty before I send it along to everyone."

Raymond reviewed the key points of the discussion once again. "So, the first inukshuk, if you all agree, will be an overall supervisory profile identifying all of the key skills that we'll be discussing based on your individual choices. Train staff, and coach and develop staff. Terry, I know you're keen on those two from what you've told me. Next, optimizing teams, that goes along with your improving work processes objective, if I'm not mistaken Sylvie. Let's see, motivate staff and maintain discipline, that's Gary's. All right? Good. Gary, we'll put you down for clarifying expectations since you brought the issue up. Marty, your skills are managing change and communicating through listening and presenting. And, as for me, I want to focus on applying facilitation skills and managing results through effective meetings. Now keep in mind that we'll be examining each of these skills in turn using an individual inukshuk. Is everybody O.K. with that?"

There were smiles and nods all around. Everyone agreed on the skill areas that Raymond had defined for them as part of a profile of key supervisory skills, or "super skills," as Gary had called them. Raymond then tucked the napkin that he'd been working on in his shirt pocket, patting it as he put it away. Afterwards, they talked about various things not related to supervision and enjoyed the time they spent together. The time they shared with each other every other Thursday was a chance for them to talk about supervisory issues and share experiences over a fine lunch and delicious tea.

15

At the Plant

Over the next few days, Gary set about preparing for his meeting with his manager, Jim Ferris. He studied production reports, schedules, and all of the data that crossed his desk. He reviewed job descriptions for all of his staff, and made notes on those areas where he needed clarification from the Human Resources Group. He called Jim Ferris and asked him to set aside an hour to review his job in light of the 30% production target. The meeting was set for 7:30 a.m. Tuesday. The days passed quickly. Ferris arrived on time and looked in good spirits. Gary had brought coffee.

"Jim, I've looked at all the reports I've been getting and wanted to review them along with your expectations. Before we get into the details, I'd really like to hear your comments on what your expectations are for my job. That way, I'll be able to keep on target. What are the key parts of my job from your point of view."

Ferris smiled, and opened the lid of his coffee. Gary passed some sugar and cream over to him. "Good," Jim said. " We're always so busy that we don't often get a chance to zero in on the basics. The first thing, I guess, is the production target, and the schedules that will take us there. Production and quality are the two areas that are up front for us. We've got quality standards in place and unfortunately it seems to me that we're always struggling to ensure quality. Production without quality won't make the cut. Rework is too expensive. Those areas are crucial. Let's begin with those as major expectations. I want you to meet our 30% production goal without sacrificing quality. Any rework that we have to do really costs us. I really want you to keep our costs down. So, as far as I'm concerned, production, quality, and costs, these three areas are really important to your job and mine. These are my expectations. I want you to meet production goals, and schedules, keep quality up by meeting our standards, and keep costs down by staying within budget. Got it?"

"Sure do," Gary said, jotting down Jim Ferris's comments on a lined, yellow notepad in front of him. "What about the people side of things? What do you expect there?"

Ferris seemed a bit surprised by the question and paused for a moment. Gary sensed that he hadn't thought much about it.

"Yeah, you're right to ask me that. Without the people, we can't do it. I want you to keep them motivated. I know that's not as easy as it sounds. We can't offer any special incentives because there's no budget for it. But, we're paying them a decent wage and our benefits are competitive with the industry. That's what HR tells me. Just keep them happy, whatever way you can. If you can't keep them happy, keep them in line. You're in charge of discipline for your group. You've got to watch people like Tommy Johnson. He's slippery. He'll take you to the cleaners if he can. Watch him."

Gary continued to jot down key points. He stopped his note-taking to summarize, and secure Ferris's agreement on these points. "So, your expectations for me are to motivate staff and make sure people problems are handled."

"That's right. We've got rules we have to follow, for absenteeism, for alcohol abuse. The thing is, you're on the front line, and you have to deal with it. It's not easy, but it's what we expect from you. Are you O.K. with that?"

"It's part of the job," Gary answered. " I'll do it, but I need help on knowing what to do."

"I'll try to get you a day or two of training," Ferris said. "Talk to HR, and get familiar with the policies and procedures. You really need to be up on them. I know that Tommy Johnson is. He can find any loophole we have, and use it to his advantage."

"Sure thing, Jim. Can you think of anything else that's expected as part of the job?"

"Let me have a look at your job description. Hmm, it's pretty broad, but there are a few things here. Orientation and training, for instance. I want you to look after inducting new employees, showing them the ropes. And, oh yes, training.

I want you to make sure they have the training they need to operate our new equipment. I don't want anyone damaging million dollar machines because of a lack of training. That's another thing. Look after all the equipment, and let me know immediately if anything goes wrong."

Gary was writing quickly, glancing up every now and then at Ferris, and nodding. Gary was getting a much better understanding of his role. In the back of his mind he was amused at the thought that Ferris was also learning about the supervisory role through clarifying his expectations as a manager.

"Apart from that," Ferris continued, "do the planning and scheduling you need to do to keep in line with our targets. Judging from all of those reports you've got laid out in front of you, I can see you've got a handle on that. The follow through is really important. If you run into a snag, let me know right away."

"What about the work I do on the floor? Can I make changes to plans and schedules if they're not on target?"

Ferris leaned forward in his chair, his face set. "No. I don't want you to make any decisions that affect planning without my say so. Definitely not. I don't want you to make any decisions without me on that score. We've spent a lot of time in setting things up, and nobody, except me, makes any changes to our plan. The same thing goes for schedules. I mean, you decide who works the different shifts, but the schedules are mine. Got it?"

"Sure, but what happens if you're not around," Gary said. "Sometimes a decision has to be made right away, and if it's not made on the spot, bigger problems come up."

"You leave the decision-making to me. That's what they pay me for. I don't delegate decision-making. You can page me anytime, day or night. I'm always on call. Don't forget that."

Gary nodded, but he felt uncomfortable with Ferris's comment. It seemed to him that he was not being included in something that he should be involved with. It left him feeling on the out, so he decided to say something about it.

"Jim, that doesn't leave me feeling too good about how you feel about my decision-making abilities. I'm not talking about major decisions here. I'm thinking about issues that come up on the floor and need a quick decision made."

" Sorry, management makes the decisions. Period." Ferris said. "It's not just you because you're new. All the Supervisors here have to refer to management when decisions are needed."

"But some decisions are pretty minor. I'm sure you wouldn't want me paging you for every little thing," Gary said.

"Let's just do it my way, O.K.? I want to keep on top of things. We've got a major new investment on the floor, and I don't want it jeopardized." Ferris was beginning to look a little agitated. Gary noticed that Ferris's lower lip was trembling. Gary sat back in his chair and nodded.

"All right. I understand," Gary said, as Ferris was rising from his chair. Gary was determined that he'd do the best he could with the expectations he had taken from Ferris. He knew there were probably a few gaps, but his notes covered a lot of territory with the exception of decision-making. That bothered him. He wondered what the other Supers would say about the decision-making issue the next time they met at the restaurant.

Ferris stood up and tossed the empty coffee container in the wastebasket. "By the way," he said, " I like how you planned this meeting. Now you've got my expectations. It was a great idea. Get me a copy of what you write up for yourself. We may have missed something." Ferris turned and left Gary's office.

Gary examined the notes he had taken. He felt positive about it. He knew what he had to do, what was expected. The trouble was, he thought, the decision-making part of things was missing. He had all kinds of responsibilities without authority. He couldn't make decisions without Jim Ferris's go-ahead signal. It made him feel like a kid. He didn't like it, but what could he do? So much for supervisory self-esteem he thought. He resolved to do his best and set about reviewing the latest production reports before he walked the plant floor.

A few minutes later Gary was walking the floor checking his latest data with the machine operators. He was a little disgruntled with the forms being used to record data. They were more complicated than necessary. He made a mental note to check with the technical department to see if they could be simplified. He caught sight of Tommy Johnson waving him over.

"Hey bro, how's it going?"

"Not too bad, Tommy. How about yourself?"

"Much better now that I've had my fill of walleye. Best fishing trip I've had in years. Oh yeah, there's a couple of nice fillets for you in the lunch room fridge. It's wrapped in tin foil, and I put your name on it."

"Thanks Tommy, I appreciate that," Gary said. "Tommy, I noticed that you've got a lot of downtime recorded during the last few weeks. What's been the problem?"

" I don't really know. I've been following all the maintenance procedures that the technical people gave me. It just seems to cut out every now and then. Vinko's the only guy who seems to be able to get it going after a while. Check with him."

"I'll do that, but try to monitor it closely so that we can pinpoint where the problem is, O.K.?"

"I'll do that bro," Johnson said, winking at Gary. Gary noticed that a couple of machine operators at the next work station smiled at each other when they heard Johnson addressing Gary as "bro." "Don't forget about your fish," Tommy said.

Gary nodded, and remembered what Ferris had said about Johnson. He'd have to check his file with HR. He didn't want to be used by anyone regardless of their friendliness. That brought up another point. Ferris had told him about Johnson, but that had come out only through their meeting on expectations. Gary knew that he needed to communicate regularly with Ferris. That was a given. How could he be expected to do his job if he wasn't included in the communications loop with management? He'd need to address that with Ferris. What bothered him was the angry look on Ferris's face when they had talked about decision-making. If Ferris felt the same way about sharing information with him as he did about decision-making, they were going to run into trouble. He was sure of it.

Over the next few days Gary spent a lot of his time with Vinko who was an incredibly patient teacher. He was able to give Gary a crash course in how the workflow moved on the line, and most importantly, why. He explained in detail what each of the new machines did, and what the result was. Vinko showed him the connection between the report data he held in his hands and the actual items produced on the line. In Gary's mind he had never experienced better on-the-job training. Vinko took as much time as was necessary to check Gary's understanding of the concepts behind the workflow and the processes that Gary was observing on the plant floor.

What kept nagging at him, at the back of his mind, was the lack of trust that Ferris had shown in his abilities as a Supervisor. That was the issue that had surfaced. He knew it wasn't personal. Ferris felt the same way about all of his Supervisors, But that didn't make it any easier to take. If he wasn't going to be included in the communications loop with management, and if he couldn't make decisions on his own, what was the point of trying to do the best job he could? He felt like a kid again, waiting for his father to tell him what to do. He didn't like the situation he was in at all.

Thursday Dim Sum

"So that's where I'm at. Just when I'm getting a handle on things, on what has to be done, on my Supervisory skills, my manager tells me not to worry about making any decisions. As for communication, it just doesn't happen. Oh sure, he'll tell me what he thinks I have to do, and then I do it. Some communication! I might as well be a robot." Gary brushed back the lock of hair that fell across his forehead and took a big gulp of his tea.

"You know," Terry said, savoring his first shrimp dumpling, " there's a saying: 'Do the best you can, with what you have, where you are.' You gave me that one Raymond. What I'm trying to say is that even with the limitations he's put on you, you can still do the best job you can. You just have certain liabilities that he may or may not come to recognize."

"What do you mean by liabilities?"

"Well, you're not going to be able to do your job as good as you'd like to because your manager has set limits on what you can do. You can't make decisions on your own. You aren't in close communication with management. These limits are your liabilities. If you run into a problem because of them, you can point to them, and tell him that's why. Usually, that's what it takes to change things, unless the guy is a control freak. For some people, bossing others and playing the big shot, is what work is all about. A sad tale, but true. If that happens to be the case, you might want to work on your resume." Terry licked his fingers.

Raymond smiled sadly. "Terry's got a point. Hopefully, your manager has the best interests of the company at heart. Some fellows have big egos, and it's hard for them to share things and take input from subordinates. Not all managers, but I've met my share of the ones who don't listen."

Sylvie smiled brightly at Gary. "Look on the positive side. Like Terry said, 'do the best you can,' and you'll be all right, no matter what happens. As Supers, there are things that we have no control over. We can try to influence those areas, but they're outside of our scope of control. So, you've got to find out just how much control you do have. You're still new. They probably want to check you out before they allow you to make decisions that cost them money."

Gary leaned back in his chair, hearing it creak beneath him. "You know, I wish I didn't feel so squeezed in by both sides, by management and regular staff. I have to communicate up and down. No matter what you do, you can't seem to please everyone."

'Welcome to the club," Marty said.

"Yeah, the Super club," Gary answered warmly.

At the Plant

The door to Gary's office suddenly burst open, and there, before him, stood Jim Ferris, out of breath, and his face a mask of angry frustration.

"What happened? We... we don't have any spare parts left. Our inventory is gone. It's all gone. Why, why didn't you order more?" The veins on Jim Ferris's temple seemed about to burst. He was clearly one of the angriest men Gary had ever encountered. Gary stood up quickly, defensively.

"You didn't give me any authority to make that decision. I told you last Wednesday we were running out of parts." Gary was a little surprised at Ferris's belligerence, but he wasn't intimidated. Just behind Ferris stood Vinko Grubisic, his face pale and agitated. He looked so small behind Ferris's looming figure.

"Yeah, yeah, but I don't have to tell you everything to do, do I? I mean, if we're out of inventory, we can't do anything." Ferris's white shirt was peppered with perspiration.

"So you're telling me I can order inventory. I didn't know that before. I thought you looked after it. That was my understanding," Gary said.

"Well, now you know."

"Good. Jim, I want to make sure there are no more misunderstandings. Can we go over some of the expectations for the job again. I've made up a short one-page list, and I need to get it right."

"Sure, sure, but not right now. I've got to get a whole lot of things straightened out, and I don't have the time right now."

"Can we make an appointment?" Gary asked.

"Look, I'll call you tomorrow when I've got a minute, O.K.?" Ferris was out the door before Gary had a chance to say anything.

The phone rang. Instinctively, Gary shuddered. It hadn't been a good day. He listened as the Human Resources Manager voiced a complaint about Tommy Johnson. She wanted to see Gary immediately. Before Gary left his office, he thought about the other supervisors and their conversations together over lunch. He resolved to do his best. He's taken on this job, and he wanted to see it through. On his way out the door he glanced at the photo of Carly on his desk and smiled.

Inukshuk One: Supervisory Profile

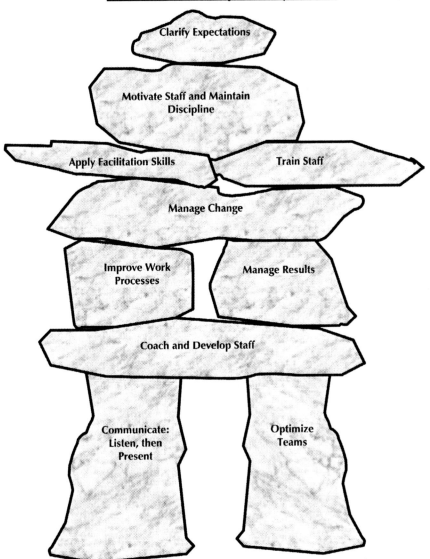

Super Skill: Apply Facilitation Skills

Profile Two: Raymond Tang

Raymond Tang is keen on making sure that his staff can apply facilitation techniques to problems encountered in his department. He encourages his staff to apply facilitative techniques such as brainstorming to arrive at the best possible solution. What he is also trying to do is to find the best way to coach and prepare his staff in finding the right solutions to any and all problems that arise. Nearing retirement, he wants his people to learn continuously and to utilize unconventional approaches to problems that confront them. Once a week he has a one-hour staff meeting where he begins to encourage a facilitative mindset among his staff.

Thursday Dim Sum

With a few deft strokes, Raymond Tang drew the outline of an inukshuk on the blank sheet of paper in front of him. It was simply entitled **Inukshuk One: Supervisory Profile**. Within the outline of the top stone of the figure, he printed two words in bold letters: Clarify Expectations. That's where it begins he thought. Within each of the stone blocks of the inukshuk drawing he printed the supervisory skills that had been selected for discussion at the last dim sum luncheon. This would give Gary Clark a good framework for his new supervisory role. He hoped the other supervisors found it useful as well. He'd find out soon enough, he thought, over noodles and tea.

Raymond Tang was only a few months away from retirement, but he was still actively engaged in his work. He didn't believe in taking it easy and coasting when there was so much fun to be had in solving problems with people. He was the kind of man who from an early age had enjoyed taking clocks apart to see how they worked. He loved the excitement of problem solving especially when it was shared with other people. Raymond loved to walk in the countryside in his spare time. He would often try to anticipate cloud formations after hearing the local weather report.

He was a practical, congenial man whose core belief about the world was summed up in his father's favorite saying: "do the best you can, with what you have, where you are." A strong believer in continuous learning, it had been Raymond's idea to use dim sum lunches as the occasion for discussions on supervisory issues. It seemed to him that nothing was finer than a good conversation with friends over a great meal.

"Marty, maybe you can help me out," Raymond said. "You've been working with a consultant on your change issue. You've been at workshops that used a facilitator. I'm curious about how things went. How was the workshop facilitated?"

Gary looked across the table at Marty, and then back again to Raymond. He looked puzzled. "Before you start Marty, tell me what you mean by 'facilitation.'"

"Basically, my understanding is that facilitation is a way of structuring discussion and making things easier to understand. The facilitator guides things along, sort of leading without taking over. The trick is to get others to assume responsibility and take the lead."

"That's just what I want to do," Raymond said. "I want others to take over the lead when it comes to things like problem solving. I'm retiring soon, and I don't want to leave

28

my team and my department up in the air. The trouble is, I don't know how to go about it, to coach them."

Marty motioned to a waitress to bring over some more tea by holding up a teapot. The restaurant was crowded now, and there was a pleasant, busy din in the air as people enjoyed their lunch.

"The important thing is that the facilitator does the job well. Getting a good definition of the goal and specific objectives really has to be done well. A good session will start with that and then it's a question of guiding the discussion and keeping it on track. Everyone's contributions have to be noted on a flip chart or whiteboard very quickly so the process doesn't stall."

"So, do you think it's the best way to go about problem solving?" Raymond asked.

"Yeah, I think so, but facilitation can cover a lot of other things too. It can help a group make high-quality decisions in no time flat. It can identify issues, secure commitment, uncover obstacles, all kinds of different things. It's a structured process that uses different methods and tools to get at what's needed by a group."

Sylvie tilted her head slightly to one side, unconsciously. Marty had observed that she always had that mannerism when she had a question about something. Years of police investigations had taught him something.

"Sylvie, a question?"

"If facilitation can do all the things you say it can, we should all be trained as facilitators. What do you think?"

"I think so. It's a key part of the supervisory role, and it makes supervision a heck of a lot easier. But it's not as easy as I've made it sound. Facilitators can run into problems. They have to manage conflict, for instance. Someone in the group may have a hidden agenda. A lot of different things can come up and a facilitator has to be able to know what to do."

"So," Raymond said, "where do we go next? You've told us about the facilitator's role. It seems to me from what you've said that giving the right kind of feedback is essential, both

29

in what's said, and what's recorded. The facilitator leads and guides without taking over. Am I correct in saying that?"

"Right on," Marty answered. "One basic rule is to make sure to differentiate between process and content. The facilitator manages the process. Process, remember, has to do with how things are being discussed, the tools, methods, and framework used. It's also about group dynamics, the tone of the group. Most meetings totally ignore process and focus on content instead. It's easy to do. Most people are task-focused. They want to solve the problem or get the job done. What they forget about are the processes being used. After all, processes are unseen and silent for the most part. A facilitator looks after the process parts, and leaves the content to the participants. He's neutral on the content. He's not playing his part if he's trying to influence the content. Follow me?"

"So," Raymond said, "how should the facilitator act, what are the behaviors that mark a skilled facilitator?"

Marty looked at the ceiling for a moment, summoning memories of good facilitators he had observed. Then he leveled his gaze at Raymond and began. "Involvement is one of the keys. A facilitator has to involve people, encouraging everyone to get in on the discussion. It's about receiving and giving feedback. That means listening really well, keeping open, and staying neutral. He has to keep focused on objectives, checking on the time available and pacing himself accordingly. It's about flexibility too, changing the approach when it's needed."

Raymond was jotting down the things Marty was saying. When he finished, he put down his pencil and looked across the table at Marty.

"Marty, have you got some facilitation technique that I can start with? You know the situation I'm in. I need ways to develop a problem-solving mindset in my staff. I'll be retiring soon, and I don't want to leave them unprepared."

"I think you know more about problem solving than I do. But as far as a mindset goes, I'd suggest a few tools that everyone can use. I've got a few favorites, and maybe we can start with those. Once they're mastered, they can be used for all kinds of purposes. Anybody have any suggestions? I know I'm not the only Super here who uses facilitation tools. "

Sylvie's eyes shone with eagerness. Marty smiled at her. "Well, I really like brainstorming," she said. "It's been around a long time, I know, but it still works if you know how to use it. The basic rules haven't changed. Get everyone involved in generating as many ideas as possible within a certain time limit. Don't evaluate any of the ideas until everyone's finished. Record the ideas that people give you in point form on a flip chart. Keep things moving, and be funny and creative when you can."

"I couldn't have said it better," Marty said.

"Nice going Sylvie, but I've got some shy people in my department. You couldn't get them to say 'Boo!' in front of a group even if they saw a ghost. I'm not kidding. It's just the way it is." Gary remembered that it wasn't so long ago that he felt the same way. He suffered agonies when he had to make a presentation, and until recently had experienced difficulties when speaking at company meetings.

"There's a technique, a variation on brainstorming, that I use to encourage shy people to contribute their ideas. It also serves to level the playing field when you have one or two people who dominate the others in a regular brainstorming session." Marty retrieved a yellow pad of sticky notes from his pocket. "Once we've got a topic to generate ideas on, I pass out several sticky note bits of paper to everyone. I ask them to jot down their ideas. I give them anywhere from three to ten minutes to come up with as many ideas as they can. No names on the paper, just ideas. Once that's done, I ask them to fold their small papers up and place them in the center of the table. Then I mix up the papers and ask each person to take back as many as they put in. If they happen to get one of their own ideas back, they exchange it with someone. The next step is take five to ten minutes to build on the original idea on the slip of paper pulled from the pile. If you want, you can pass on the slips to a third person to generate even more ideas.

31

From there, you ask everyone to read out the suggestions. The ideas are discussed, and then a recorder prints them on a flip chart. It's a great process when you need anonymity. It gives people the freedom to express their ideas."

"Not bad, not bad at all," Raymond said. "I like the idea of brainstorming, and I use it a lot. I really haven't thought about using the anonymous version, but I think I will. The thing is, I've always had a bit of trouble deciding what to do next. What I mean is, what to do with all of the ideas generated? How do I narrow it down and get everyone to agree on the short list?"

"Dots. Sticker dots. That's what I use," Marty said.

"I don't follow you," Raymond queried.

"There are a lot of fancier ways to narrow things down, but I like the sticker dot method. After we've generated a lot of ideas that are posted on flip chart paper, I give everyone three or four dots. I ask them to place a dot beside each idea they especially favor. Then I tally up the results. That's a quick and dirty way to prioritize the brainstormed items. Once we've narrowed things down, we can decide what we're going to do next."

"I like it," Raymond said, his eyes wrinkling at the corners in little smiles.

"What if you can't find sticker dots?" Gary asked.

"Good point," Marty answered, noticing a few broad smiles sprouting around the table after Gary's remark. "Some of you might laugh, but training budgets are incredibly tight these days. Look, if you can't get the nice-to-have stuff, improvise. Get everyone to go up to flip chart sheets and, with a felt tip marker or whatever is handy, ask them to put a checkmark beside the ideas they like. Not fancy, but it works."

Raymond laughed, giving a thumbs-up to Gary.

"Hey Raymond," Marty said, "you're not the only one who can draw. I want to show you something." Marty was sketching some lines on one of the napkins. He held it up for everyone to see.

"Well, what does it look like to you?"

"It looks like an arrow with some lines attached," Gary offered.

"Oh c'mon now," Marty said, "surely you can all see it's a fishbone."

"We'll give you the benefit of the doubt," Terry said.

"Fair enough then. Raymond, this is one of the best problem-solving techniques that I know of. The head of the fish here, this triangle, is the problem being analyzed. It's the effect that people can observe. Now, the fishbones, the lines running from the central line, or backbone, are the causes. I call these lines the cause categories. They can vary depending on what's being analyzed. The common ones though include categories like people, machinery, methods, materials, and the environment. There's no set number. These categories are the ribs of the fish. Once you've determined what they are, you can start brainstorming all of the causes for each rib. Do you follow me?"

Marty was holding up the napkin in front of his chest. An elderly man at the next table started smiling at him and nodding vigorously. The old man pointed to a fish tank located against the back wall of the restaurant.

Marty chuckled. "See, that guy knows that this is a fish."

"I like the simplicity of it," Raymond said thoughtfully. "It's got a lot of functionality. You can zero in on the causes you need to look at."

Sylvie nodded in agreement. "I know I'll be able to use that fishbone diagram with my teams. But just one question Marty."

"What's that?"

"The fish- was it grouper or sole?"

Marty groaned. "You'll never know."

At the Office

Back at his office, Raymond thought over the problem solving approaches he had learned over dim sum. Marty had called the techniques he had outlined 'facilitation.' Raymond realized that he had been instinctively using these techniques for years. Now, it was important to make certain that his staff knew how to apply the techniques in a conscious way. He needed to coach them. He needed to encourage in them a way of thinking that was fundamental to team tasks such as problem solving. Raymond was sitting quietly in his office and staring blankly at the white wall in front of him. Before any technique, he mused, they required a mind set, a framework that could encompass any problem.

As he reviewed his own experience and thought about his approach to problem solving, he realized that patterned thinking was at the heart of it. Each of the processes in the office functioned in routine, systematic ways, ways that were patterned. He thought about the many times when problems occurred that disrupted the patterned functioning of the workflow. Whenever that happened, Raymond had stepped back and analyzed the situation. He thought of it as his troubleshooting mode. He would examine the situation and break it down into its component parts. Then he would systematically review each of the parts until the problem was pinpointed. It was all about analysis, he thought. Analysis was the fundamental method used in troubleshooting. Most of his time was really spent on troubleshooting, rather than what he considered as true problem solving. Troubleshooting was simply a building block towards higher level problem solving.

The whiteness of the wall in front of him was like a screen for his thinking. Troubleshooting, he realized, was based on asking the right questions. Questions were a way of probing, useful in identifying the problem. The backdrop to any problem was the pattern behind it, the pattern that had been disrupted because of the problem. He remembered the questions that he used as prompts when he was troubleshooting: Where is the problem located? Where can we see the problem? Where did it first happen? Is the problem a part of a sequence? Who is involved in the situation? Raymond realized that when he concentrated in this way, it was similar to the meditations his father had instructed him in when he was a boy. He knew it was going to be difficult to impart that basic mind set when he coached his staff, but he wanted to try. It would be the best legacy he could leave behind when he retired.

"Today's meeting," Raymond said to the five people convened around the table, "is about facilitation. I want to make it a standard practice to examine different tools, different facilitative techniques, that we can use together in our work here. Facilitation is just a fancy word for using analytical tools to get at results. It's a process and that's where I want to start."

Raymond then gave an orientation speech outlining the rationale and purposes of facilitation. He spoke about developing a toolbox of facilitative techniques. He was very serious in his manner and clearly focused. All five team members were impressed with his commitment and the obvious enthusiasm he conveyed in his voice and gestures. Some of them wondered if he was ready for retirement.

"The thing is," Raymond concluded, "by applying these facilitation skills we can move quickly to the results we've identified. By practicing them, we'll be both disciplined and creative. I'll be giving you an overview of these tools over the next few meetings. Each of you will have many opportunities to practice the role of facilitator. Any comments or questions?"

"Aren't you retiring in a few months?" Sarah Mifflen asked.

"Yes."

"Boy, no rest for the wicked," she said. "I mean most people are coasting at this stage of the game, but you're going full bore all the way."

Raymond laughed. "I've always enjoyed your turn of phrase, but I've never thought of myself as 'wicked.'"

"By 'wicked,' I mean really good," Sarah said.

"Well that's good to know."

"I guess you want to make sure the team can still function when you're gone, I mean retired."

"Of that I have no doubt," Raymond replied. "I think our team will work a lot more effectively when meetings are facilitated. Remember, it's about discipline and creativity, and the facilitation process can accommodate both."

"Without you around to take the flak, we're going to run into a lot of resistance," Sarah said.

"That's for sure," Martin Jones said.

Raymond's eyes sparkled with anticipation. "Let's start with that then," he said. "Resistance. The tool we'll use is called force field analysis. It's a way of examining positive and negative forces working on an issue."

"One of our goals is to increase the departmental budget. Can we use that in this force field analysis?" Martin asked.

"Why not? Let's begin with identifying the driving forces? These driving forces 'drive' the change we want, in this case, an increased budget." Raymond stood and walked over to the white board. He drew a vertical line down the middle of the white board. "This line represents the status quo, how things are right now. To the left will be the driving forces. To the right we'll identify the restraining forces, the elements or factors preventing or obstructing us from getting the increased allocation we want. Now we have to brainstorm the forces in either direction. Martin, start us off."

"O.K., one of the drivers is the need for new project management software."

"I know the Vice President supports an increase. She's told us that often enough in staff meetings."

"We can utilize extra funds for internal training. We haven't kept up with our professional development. We need that to capitalize on new project opportunities."

"We're often called upon to help other departments with their projects. New software will give us that capability."

Raymond drew horizontal arrows with a blue marker on the left side of the vertical line to indicate the driving forces. Above each arrow he printed a few words indicating the idea behind it. He paused for a few moments while others gave additional comments, and then he listed these in the same manner.

"What about restraining forces?" Raymond asked. "What's holding us back from securing additional funds?"

"The Chief Accountant has asked all of the departments to cut back a minimum of ten per cent."

"Upgrades to the system we have now might counter the need for new software."

Raymond captured the restraining forces with red, horizontal arrows drawn on the right side of the white board, opposite the blue arrows. With each additional comment and idea from his team, the white board was soon filled up.

"Now we have to prioritize both sides of the board. We have to assign a relative value to each of the arrows. We can use an A1 rating for the strongest forces, and an A, B, or C to the others, with numbers where warranted. Let's do it."

Once this phase had been completed, Raymond asked for specific actions to either strengthen or weaken the impact of each arrow. One of his team members, Sheila Charles, acted as a recorder and noted all of the contributions.

"Good," Raymond said. "It's a good start. We can refine this and then have some solid ideas to present to management. We'll present a good solid case for our budget increase. It'll point in the right direction, like an inukshuk."

"What's that?" Sheila asked.

"An inukshuk is an arrangement of stones piled up on one another to look like a person. The word actually means 'in the image of a person'. In the arctic, where it originated, an inukshuk serves as a directional marker in treeless horizons to help guide those who follow. I really love it as a symbol because it reminds me of our dependence on each other." Raymond picked up a black marker and drew an inukshuk in a corner of the white board that was unmarked. "That's roughly what an inukshuk looks like."

"I've seen that before," Sheila said. "On the way to my cottage up north, there are a few situated on some hills just off the highway."

Raymond smiled. "I want each of you to develop your facilitation skills. As team leaders, having capability in this area is essential. You'll use it to refine your thinking, and the thinking of people that report to you. For problem solving and decision making, the facilitative approach can't be beat. What we're talking about here is the building up of a toolbox of structured processes. When it's all said and done, facilitation is about communication, about helping groups and teams release their potential for excellence and achieve the results they want. It's nothing less."

"Boy, this sounds serious, even a little intimidating," Sheila said.

Raymond laughed. "I didn't mean to sound like a preacher, and don't worry, it won't be intimidating after you've facilitated a few sessions."

"Are the best meetings always facilitated?" Sheila asked.

"Not necessarily. You see, it depends on the purpose of the meeting. For a strictly information-sharing meeting, using facilitation tools wouldn't be effective or even meaningful. But for coming up with new ideas, or problem solving, or decision making, that's the way to go."

"And that's why you're coaching us on it, for our team meetings?"

"Yes. It's taken me a long time to realize that. There are really three key elements or aspects involved in all this. The first concerns our meetings. We have to be very clear on why we're meeting and the guidelines we use to communicate. We're looking to that, and our meetings are getting better as a result. They're not perfect, but they're getting better. The second aspect has to do with our team, and where we are in the team's development. Here again, it's just as important to think about process, about how we're handling the tasks that we've been given. Finally, there's facilitation, the structured way we approach problem solving and decision making. It's all three of those combined that can make the difference: meetings, teams, and facilitation. That's what it's all about."

"The whole is greater than the sum of its parts," Sarah chimed in, brightly.

"Right on," Raymond said, the lines around his eyes crinkling with affection.

Raymond then summarized the meeting and gave some assignments to be completed before the team met again. The mood of the team was upbeat and focused. The meeting concluded on time. Sarah stayed behind to speak with Raymond.

"We're going to miss you."

"I'm not retiring for a few months yet."

"Are you ready for it, for retirement I mean?"

"Good question. I think so, but I'll find out soon enough."

"I guess you have a lot of interests outside of work."

"A few. I enjoy photography, gardening. I like to keep busy."

"Busy? But isn't the whole point of retirement to do nothing? I mean, you've finally get a chance to play full-time. Being busy makes it sound too much like work."

"My father used to say 'like work or get work you like.' That's always made a lot of sense to me. I don't like work for work's sake, just to fill in time. No one does. I like it for what it brings out in a person and the satisfaction it gives. I can't imagine just doing nothing. That would take the fun out of life."

Sarah flashed a disarming smile and then her face changed suddenly, and was creased with doubts. "Raymond, do you really think we can get this 'facilitation' thing up and running? I mean, it's O.K. when you're around, but what about when you're not? Do you think we can do it?"

"'If you think you can or can't, you're right.' You see Sarah, I'm just full of quotes and sound bites. The thing is, you have to keep focused, clearly focused on what you're doing. Let the doubts come, and let the doubts go. Just let things take their course, but keep focused. If you do that, and do it consistently, you'll be all right. Time to go now."

"Thanks Raymond."

Inukshuk Two: Apply Facilitation Skills

Facilitate Meetings

Select Facilitation Tool

Appoint Recorder

Build Toolbox

Develop Facilitative Role

Use Problem Solving Techniques

Apply Decision Making Processes

Engage Participants Fully

Access Creativity and Discipline through Facilitative Techniques

Combine Meeting, Team, and Facilitative Processes

Super Skill: Train Staff

Profile Three: Terry Dunn

Terry Dunn has worked as a front line supervisor for ten years. New equipment and new work procedures for a retooled automotive plant are frustrating his staff. Terry is a good Supervisor, but he's unsure of what he needs to do to get his team trained and ready. He does not know where to start. Many of his staff are in need of basic training before receiving more specialized machine-based training.

At the Plant

Terry looked at himself in the washroom mirror. He saw a middle-aged, balding man, pale and slightly overweight. He wondered for a fleeting second when it was that he had lost his physical edge. He remembered a time when he was trim and when the look on his face was sharper, more alert, less jowly. His jaw line was slack and undefined. He thought that it couldn't be the aging process alone that left him with that impression. He sucked in his gut and turned away from the mirror, a little disgusted at life in general. Here he was, ten years on the job and feeling like a rookie. The plant had been completely overhauled and the production kickoff was only several weeks away. He had forty-eight people under him who needed to be trained on the new machinery, and he didn't have a clue about where to begin.

He walked across the plant floor keeping within the newly painted lines marking the safe walkway. He couldn't help but admire the scale of the operation and the bright new vision of it all. The plant was like a futuristic scenario of things to come. The place was busy and humming with the sounds of finishing touches being put on the new equipment and conveyor belts. There seemed to be a light mist in the plant air. Engineers in white hats moved in small groups from one workstation to the next. Tow trucks whizzed by, their horns signaling when necessary. Terry felt elated to be a part of it all, but he was worried. He wanted to do something, and he needed to do something to get ready for the production start-up date, but his thinking seemed paralyzed, not up to the challenge.

He needed to talk with someone and the luncheon meeting at the Jade Garden Restaurant with the other Supervisors was a full week away. His brow wrinkled tightly at the thought of waiting that long. He made his way to his office and phoned Raymond Tang for some advice.

"From what you've told me," Raymond said, " you've got to get a clear focus on what the training is meant to do. Is it addressing a problem, or an opportunity, or both?"

"My situation is pretty clear," Terry answered. " We've got all kinds of new technology and equipment. It's training that's needed."

"Well then, before you get into the details of training, focus on the big picture. Find out what was happening before the new investment in equipment, and then what should be happening once everything is up and running. What's the new equipment meant to do from a business angle? What's the production target? Zero in on the numbers. You've got to be an investigator at this stage, like Marty."

"But Raymond, that has nothing to do with training. That's management's job, the numbers thing, not mine."

"It's everybody's job. As a Super, you need to know what the training is meant to do. You have to look at what you want to happen, the targets, in order to pinpoint the training that's needed. To reach those production targets, you may also need to look at non-training issues."

Terry's pager began to sound. "Raymond, I've got to run now, but I want to talk more about this on Thursday, O.K.?"

"Sounds good. I'll look forward to seeing you there. Bye now."

Thursday Dim Sum

Terry looked a bit anxious as he explained the situation he was in to the other Supers. Raymond looked on thoughtfully, remembering their telephone conversation. He heard the same edgy tone in Terry's voice. He noticed that Terry hadn't yet eaten a single shrimp dumpling from the dim sum basket in front of him.

"Raymond, you talked to me the other day about comparing the present situation with what I want to happen. Like I said, I've got all kinds of people who need training on new machines and equipment. My problem is in knowing who needs to be trained on what. But you said that there were non-training issues that might come up when I started to look at training. What did you mean by that?"

"Well, you train people to improve performance. In your case, it sounds like a lot of people will need training on new machinery. In some situations though, it's not training that's needed. If people aren't doing their jobs properly, it could be that they're not getting the resources they need to do their jobs. If you want a person to wash a floor, you give him a mop, not a broom. There may be a few reasons for poor performance. It could be bad workflow design, the way an assembly line is set up, for instance. Then again, it might be the way people get rewarded. I'm not just talking about money. Sometimes, a simple thank you makes a world of difference." Raymond noticed Marty smiling at his last remark.

"Marty, would you agree?" Raymond asked.

"That's why I'm smiling. You know, a lot of my staff put in long hours. They don't have to do that, but they do. When

I thank them, I can see in their faces that my thanks mean something to them. It's a small thing, but small things add up over time. Of course, there are other more inventive ways of saying thank you."

Terry nodded. "I know getting thanked makes a difference to me. But, I still need to know how to go about getting my people trained. I mean, is there a system I can use to make sure I'm doing the right things?"

Raymond began to doodle on a napkin as he spoke to Terry. Sylvie, noticing this, glanced quickly at Marty and smiled.

"You've already started the system by figuring out what you want to happen," Raymond said. " You know there are production goals and business targets- these things help you to get the big picture. This first step is about analysis. The second step focuses on training. You need to zero in on exactly who will be trained, and what you expect people to do in their jobs. Knowing what people will be expected to do helps to keep you focused on what they need to learn. A lot of people get frustrated when they have to learn something they're not going to use in their work."

"Yeah," Terry said. "I can remember going to too many workshops that had no connection with the work we were doing. A few times, we were given software training before the software was installed on our computers. Think about it. It just doesn't make any sense. A lot of us had forgotten most of what we learned at the workshop by the time we got the new software program. Sylvie, could you please pass those shrimp rolls?"

"Timing is everything," Raymond said. "People want to learn something just when they need it, not before. And, what's often forgotten, they need to know why, the reason behind the training. Supervisors can motivate and spark interest by telling staff why they're getting the training. We need to link the training directly to what people do on the job. The question to ask yourself is this: what do you want the employee to know or do as a result of the training? If you can answer that, then you've got a solid basis to evaluate whether or not your training program was effective. Unless you do that, your training won't be nearly effective. You won't be able to evaluate it. It'll be like trying to nail jello to the wall. "

Terry sipped appreciatively at the chrysanthemum tea. It was amazing, he thought, to feel so good. The food, the ambience of the restaurant, his friends, it was wonderful. "It's going to take a while," Terry said, " to pinpoint the training my people need. "

"The next thing to consider," Raymond said, "is to consider the costs of training. Once you've identified who needs what type of training, and how much of it, you have to select the most cost-effective training solutions. It's a part of good business management. You have to think about the return on your training investment."

"But isn't that just the cost of the training you buy as a package," Terry said.

"That's part of it. But there's also the time involved, the labor costs, of your staff who are off the job. And what about the productivity loss? Even if you get people to fill in for your staff, that costs money. Then there's the cost of any equipment and materials that are needed. In some cases you have to rent training facilities, you have to cover the travel, accommodation, and meal costs, if training is off site. It all adds up very quickly, and you don't want any unpleasant surprises when the invoices and expense claims start to come in. You really have to plan well, and make sure you have your budget in place."

"Yeah, but Raymond I'm not an accountant. I hear what you're saying, but I don't know anything about return on investment. I wouldn't know where to begin."

"Terry, it's not rocket science. Just think about some of the financial paybacks from training. Think about downtime, for instance. If you could cut downtime by fifty per cent, that's great payback value. You could get a dollar figure from your accounting people, I'm sure. You just have to investigate a bit."

"Hmm, I was thinking about the non-financial benefits," Terry said. "You know, the attitude thing. When people develop skills, they feel better. Morale improves. You can feel it in the air."

"That's critical," Raymond said. " That kind of payback is very difficult to measure, but it has tremendous impact. Employees begin to feel that management cares."

Terry looked thoughtful for a moment. "What's going to be really difficult is the scheduling. There's so much training that needs to be done, with so many vendors, the companies who supply the training. And then there's the different shifts to think about: if a person's on the night shift, how can they attend a training session during the day? Whew, it's going to be tough."

"It's not something to do by yourself," Raymond offered. "You'll need help. It'll take a lot of planning and a good computer spreadsheet program. But I guarantee you, if you do it right, step by step, you'll meet all your production goals, and more. For instance, what is it you think you need to know about scheduling?"

"That's just the point Raymond. Dozens and dozens of people need training. Where do I start?"

"With one person, or with a group of people who need the same type of training delivered. Why don't you try listing the kinds of things you'd need to know to schedule the delivery of training?"

"When?"

"Right now. Here."

Terry took out a small notepad from his breast pocket and began to jot down what he thought was necessary to plan and schedule the delivery of training, any training that was deemed necessary once the training needs had been identified.

Terry glanced up at Raymond. "O.K., once the needs analysis is done, I've listed these elements: the training activity, the dates and times of training, the location, the instructor's name, and the trainees. Am I on the right track?"

"Sounds fine to me. The only other things you might want to add are the skills needed to take the training: what are the prerequisites? Sometimes, depending on the program, a foundation course is needed. And then the numbers involved: how many trainees to one instructor? And what about equipment? Who supplies that? If a lot of demonstrations are involved, you'd want to have a smaller number of trainees so everyone can participate under expert guidance. The other thing is the method of instruction. That's really important. Take computer training, for example. I wouldn't want to take a spreadsheet training program if I didn't have the program on my computer. What I don't need is a long lecture. I want a hands-on session where I can take something back to work right away. Use it, or lose it."

"You've got that right," Sylvie piped in. "After all we're not kids. We need to learn something we can use right away. A lot of companies forget about that. They think they can give you a course a few months before you need to use it. As if anyone can remember for that long."

Terry nodded in agreement. "Raymond, I'm not sure I understand about the prerequisites. What did you mean?"

"Well, I was thinking about the skills or experience trainees need before they can take the training. A person can't benefit from training if it's too advanced for them. Sometimes foundation courses are needed. For instance, if an employee is expected to understand job specifications as a regular part of their job, they probably need a course in blueprint reading. You can't take that for granted."

"Yeah, I see," Terry said, taking another sip of the fragrant tea that had just been served. "It's a whole new way of thinking... systematic and focused."

"Yes," Raymond said. "But the real challenge is in deciding the method of instruction that you choose. Not all people learn in the same way. Some prefer the traditional classroom approach, others like small groups, and still others prefer individualized on-the-job training. You have to try to accommodate individual learning styles when you can. You also have to take a good, hard look at content, whatever it is you want your people to learn. The content may call for a lecture approach, discussion, an on-the-job demonstration, or quite possibly a combination of some or all of these methods. The important thing is to think about these various methods and to use the ones that get the learning results you want. After all, you want the learning to stick. You want your learners to bring their learning back to the job."

Terry leaned forward in his chair. "I've got a lot to think about. It makes sense to me. I sure hope it makes sense to management. This is going to take a lot of time, and I'm not sure whether they'll be open to the scope of it all. Do you know what I mean?"

"You've got a selling job to do. If you can show positive results of the training investment to them, you'll have it made." Raymond tapped sharply on the tabletop with his finger to emphasize his point.

Terry smiled. "I didn't think a Supervisor had to be a salesman as well as a superman."

"Or a Superwoman," Sylvie said, her eyes smiling.

"Yes, or a superwoman," Terry agreed.

"You've got to sell the idea of training because that's time away from the job that your employees are paid to do. Somebody's got to fill in for them, and that costs money, production time. There's the time that people are being trained off-the-job in the classroom or shop. Then there's the time that they're being trained on-the-job. It all adds up. Managers want a return on their investment, and so do you, as the first line of management."

"But, from what you've said already, if I've done a solid needs analysis based on training requirements, that's the biggest part of the selling job, right?"

"Yes, but then, after the training, you've got to evaluate."

"How do I do that?"

Raymond took a clean napkin and drew what looked to Terry to be a set of stairs with four steps. On each of the steps he wrote a word. Then he turned the napkin around so that

Terry could easily see the words on the steps. "You've got to set out your criteria for evaluation before training begins," Raymond said. "The first step or level is focused on what will be evaluated. That's the content of your training, whatever it is, the training activity. This will tell you if the training method you selected was appropriate for your employees. Did they like it? The next level also focuses on whether or not learning took place based on training objectives. If the training was successful, then employees will be able to do their job better-that's the third step. And, if you take this a little further, you'll be able to assess whether or not the training met the needs you listed early on under the problems and opportunities of your needs analysis. Everything is connected Terry, and this level will finally let you know the impact that training had for your company."

" You'll have to draw one of your inukshuks for me, O.K.?" Terry asked.

"I'll do that," Raymond said. "Just remember the steps or levels: training activity, learning, job performance, and results. The whole concept was the brainchild of a fellow named Donald Kirkpatrick. It's not fancy, but it makes sense."

Sylvie cleared her throat. "Raymond, there's just one thing. Who does the evaluation?"

"Good question. Who does what? Training activities are evaluated by the trainees and the trainer. The same thing is true with the second level, the learning level. The supervisor's turn to evaluate the trainee comes up at the job performance level. Finally, the overall impact of training, the results, are evaluated by senior management. How each of the levels is evaluated, and when, will differ too. Those are things you have to think about."

"I don't understand," Terry said.

"Well, at the end of a course or workshop, there's usually a workshop evaluation sheet. Sometimes there's a discussion between the trainer and trainees on the value and usefulness of the training. The first level, the training activity level, is evaluated like that, and it usually happens at the end or near the end of the training. The second level, learning, is also evaluated the same way. Keep in mind that evaluation of the third level, the job performance level, usually happens about a month after the actual training is completed. Your management group will evaluate the results and impact of the training anywhere from six months to a year after the training is over. That's your final and fourth level."

At the Plant

Maggie Shanks from the Human Resources Group sat across from Terry in his office on the plant floor. Terry had asked her to help him with record keeping for all of the training activities on the floor. Maggie was a short, compact woman whose brisk manner of walking matched the frank manner with which she spoke.

"You've got dozens of training activities going on at the same time," Maggie said as she leafed through the course outlines on Terry's cluttered desk. "We've got to simplify things. There's just too much information in formats that we can't access quickly. Do you know what I mean?" Maggie asked.

"Do I," Terry replied. "I've been swamped with all of these different course outlines from the training suppliers. All of the information seems relevant. I don't know what to cut."

"Well, we've got to simplify, that's clear. So, let's take all of the need-to-know information and put it into a matrix, so we can see whatever it is we need to see at a glance." Maggie pushed the pile of paper over to Terry and went up to the whiteboard attached to the wall. "Just give me some of the main headings, and we'll see if we can come up with our own format, O.K.?"

"Sure thing. Here goes: course title, the machine type on the floor that the training is linked to, the instructor or provider of training, the number of course training hours, and the position the training is for. Got that?"

"Ditto. I've abbreviated things a bit, but this is a good first take on it," Maggie said. Across the top of the whiteboard,

Terry saw the categories he had given her. Then, slowly they began filling in the matrix with actual names and other descriptors such as the anticipated number of training hours.

"It's good to be able to see everything at a glance," Terry said when they finished.

"It's a start," Maggie said. "We can use this matrix format for keeping track of training on the floor too, for on-the-job training. That way people will be able to see where they are in terms of their training requirements. Keep in mind that we'll also need to keep it in synch with the shift schedule, who's working on what shift."

" Yup. Looks good, very good," Terry said.

Within a few days the training plan was finalized and training began in earnest. The matrices he had developed with Maggie Shanks were a godsend. At a glance he could see who was being trained on each shift and where. He liked its simplicity. One of the toughest managers had complimented him on "the transparency of the approach to training." He praised Terry for keeping an eye on the "big picture" and company profitability. Terry had taken a lot of complex information about training and made it accessible and understandable across different functions and levels of the organization. The training plan had also helped him to justify the expense of training in fundamentals such as blueprint reading. Terry had argued that not everyone had received formal training in the basics and that downtime in many instances was due to misinterpreting specs. "A million dollar machine running idle because someone hasn't been shown what certain symbols mean on a spec sheet is something that shouldn't happen."

Now, as Terry made his rounds on the floor, he began to realize that training had a positive affect on morale. He recognized this fact when he spoke to one of his senior machine operators, Vince Elliot.

"Well Vince, what do you think of all this training we're doing? Is it helping the new people?"

"I can't speak for them. You'll have to ask them. But, it's making a difference to me. I can do my job better now that

I can read the specs." Vince rubbed his grizzled chin as he spoke and threw a glance across the plant to the engineering office on the second floor. "Those guys are finally starting to make sense. Especially now, that they seem to be listening to us."

"What do you mean?" Terry asked.

"Well, they're taking the new training alongside us. The new machinery has to be customized in a few ways to handle the workflow. Even the vendor instructors giving us the training know that. We're giving the engineers our input, and they're listening to us. That didn't happen before. We just had to do things their way no matter how stupid it was."

Terry laughed. "I'm glad you're happy with it."

Vince rubbed his chin and smiled mischievously. "I'm glad that you're happy that I'm happy."

Terry shook his head, chuckling under his breath. "Forget it."

Thursday Dim Sum

Terry had just recounted the development of his training plan, the tracking matrices, and the positive responses he had gotten from his team. All of the Supers liked results, and they were eager to learn from Terry's experience.

"So what's the hardest part?" Gary asked, refilling Terry's cup with the piping hot chrysanthemum tea.

"Getting started," Terry shot back without even thinking. "Just deciding to do it. I mean you can have the best plan in the world, but you have to begin it. Just do it."

"Procrastination, as my irascible granddad used to say," Marty chimed, "has driven more men and women to hell than whiskey."

"Sounds like your grandpa would have been compatible with my grandma, but we won't get into that," Sylvie said. "What I want to know is what I can use. Terry, do you have some sort of template for your training plan? It could save all of us a lot of time if you do."

" I do indeed," Terry responded. "I'll e-mail the template to all of you along with the inukshuk Raymond has developed for it. I've got to tell you all that Raymond here is the mastermind behind the training plan. He's the kingpin."

"Stop it Terry. All that praise will go to my head." Raymond sipped at his tea, savoring the flavor he had remembered from his earliest childhood.

"What I've learned from Raymond is simple and yet elegant like one of his inukshuks. In fact, each of the inukshuks is a template for a particular skill. If you follow the directions, the skills, listed on the inukshuk, it can take you where you want to go."

Marty leaned forward resting his elbows against the edge of the table. "Like anything, it's the approach you take that makes the difference. Take supervision. We've been focusing on systematic approaches to effective supervision. Each inukshuk we've developed in our conversations together contains a systematic approach to the mastery of a supervisory skill."

Sylvie nodded. "And you don't really know a thing until you've practiced every part of it thoroughly."

"Right on," Gary agreed.

"It's important," Terry began, "to think in terms of systems, of systematic approaches to supervision, but you've always got to be mindful of the human element involved. You've got to treat people with respect and dignity. Without that, the best systems fail."

"That's the key to successful supervision, I think," Sylvie said. "Systematic supervision, but with a heart."

"Yeah," Marty said. "That's why I like the inukshuk drawings. They sum it all up and give direction. They point the way. We all know that the way we supervise will be different. We're different personalities in different work environments, but the fundamental skills are the same."

When the Supervisors were leaving the restaurant, Marty turned to Terry and said, "Hey, have you been working out? You look leaner and meaner especially in profile."

Terry had in fact lost most of his paunch over the past three months. He had joined a fitness center and hired a personal trainer. He walked at least an hour each day to and from work. He felt fit and enjoyed it.

"Thanks. I've been trying."

"Well, keep it up. And once you're ready, e-mail an inukshuk drawing to me of the key skills involved, O.K.?"

Terry beamed. "I'll do that."

Inukshuk Three : Train Staff

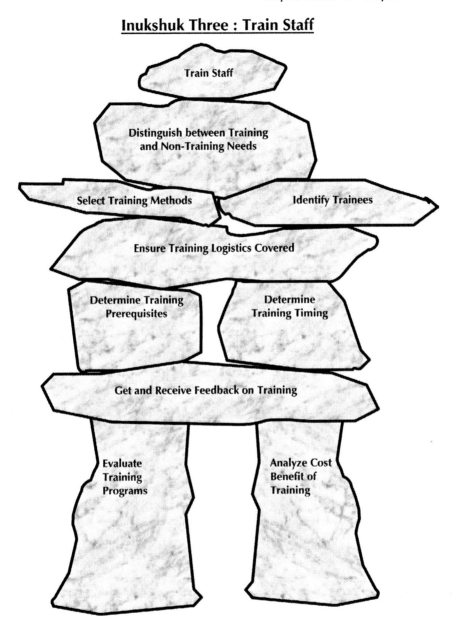

Super Skill: Manage Change

Profile Four: Marty Hessler

Marty Hessler is a front line supervisor – a non commissioned officer – for a provincial police force. He has been asked to implement a new electronic file management system in his detachment. It will replace a much older, paper-based information system. Technicians have already installed the new software, and the expectation from Headquarters is crystal clear: have the new system up and running within a month. Marty is worried about the reaction from his subordinates. They are skeptical of directives and initiatives coming from the "ivory tower," officers no longer familiar with front line policing. His staff has watched change initiatives come and go, like management fads: first it was decentralization followed by centralization followed by decentralization. He does not know where to begin.

At the Office

Marty Hessler was sitting in the small cubicle that was his office and feeling very anxious. He had been tapping a pencil against the metal edge of his desktop for five minutes running, and he wasn't even aware of it. It was up to him to break the news to his staff about the new software system that was now installed in the detachment computers, a system that he knew nothing about. He was told that it was going to revolutionize information management, and that it signaled a change in police work similar to the change in moving from the horse to the vehicle.

Apart from the hype and the new icon on his desktop screen, Marty knew nothing about the new software program. Just like Headquarters, he thought, to dump this thing on him with so little warning. It was an unknown quantity, like a pig in a poke, he thought. Maybe it would pass quickly like so many HQ fads that came and went. But still, he was told to have his people using it within a month. Marty swallowed hard and wondered where to begin. He needed to know what the new program could do before he could talk to his staff about it. The technical people who installed it could supply him with that information. He also needed to think about training people on the new system, but he knew that something else was missing.

Marty thought about his staff. They didn't suffer fools or foolish initiatives easily. If they didn't like the program, there might be resistance. He had to think about that, about how he might counter the resistance if it came up. He sat back in his chair and thought about what was happening now. Paper-reporting, paper files-that was the issue. The new program would change all that. People would input data directly into computers, at least that's how he understood it. When he thought about Steve and Gerry, he grimaced. They were a couple of years from retirement and refused to do data entry. He remembered Gerry saying "Look, I'm an investigator, not a clerk. The secretaries can do the data entry thing. That's not my job. I'm a cop." The more he thought about it, the more he realized that he needed more information. He was speculating on something he didn't know enough about. He grabbed his telephone directory and decided to make a few calls before he went any further.

"Don't worry Marty. We'll give your people training on the program. It's not going to be a sink or swim thing like it's been in the past. You just let me know the best time for my trainer to come in, and I'll set things up, O.K.?"

Marty was speaking on the telephone with Steve Harwood, an HQ Coordinator that he had worked with before.

"The thing is," Marty said, " it's not the training so much that I'm worried about. It's getting everyone to buy into it. One of the e-mails your office sent up here said that the change involved was like when policing moved from the horse to the car. Now that's mega-change as I see it. A lot of the staff here aren't that comfortable with inputting data into a computer. They're worried about losing it, and stuff like that. Some of them are close to retirement and may see it as just another flash in the pan. And another thing, some of the clerical staff, the ones who are inputting data now, are worried about their jobs. There are quite a few things that need to be talked about before training starts."

"Let me look into it Marty," Steve said with just the barest trace of anger in his voice. " I know some of the staff here have been talking about addressing the change issue, but you know how it is. We've got operational priorities and we can't be mollycoddling people. If you run into trouble, let me know. I can come down there and lay down the law. People either buy in, or they buy out. This thing has got to work, and it will, whether they like it or not."

Marty had heard the anger and the menace in Steve's voice, and he shook his head. Steve didn't get it. The old command and control approach wouldn't work anymore. People were different now. Marty knew that instinctively. The world and policing had changed, and a different way was needed. He looked forward to discussing his problem with the other Supers at the upcoming lunch. He crumpled a piece of paper he had been doodling on, and threw it like a miniature basketball into the wastebasket a few yards from his chair. It landed on the edge of the basket and then fell to the floor.

Thursday Dim Sum

"Well, Marty, I'd say you need to get someone to spend a little time before training starts to talk about change," Sylvie said, sipping at the tea she held in her hand. "I mean," she continued, " it's necessary. People need to know why there's going to be a change, the reasons behind it, and how it will affect them. You can use communication to squelch rumours right away, before they circulate like a virus."

Around them, the lunchtime atmosphere was bustling with everyone enjoying themselves.

"Sounds good, but who's going to do it. I mean the person who comes in to talk about change needs to have some credibility, or you might as well forget the whole thing," Marty said, his forehead wrinkled with the prospect of how his staff would react to someone coming into the detachment to talk about change.

"Sure you need credibility," Sylvie said, "but why not cover all the territory. Bring in someone who can talk about change in general, and then a member who can talk about details that everyone can relate to. A team approach. If you do it that way, you can cut down on the resistance to the whole thing that you're worried about."

"I like the idea Sylvie," Marty said, his face suddenly bright and enthusiastic. "Now, to try and sell it to Headquarters, that'll be the tough part. They see it as a training issue. As far as change goes, you either buy into it, or you get out. At least that's the way they talk. It's different when you've got a roomful of members in front of you."

Sylvie sat thoughtfully for a few moments and then looked up. "Ask them if they'll consider a pilot session on change. This pilot session will be about change and the highlights of the software program. It won't involve any training. One of the trainers can be a member familiar with the new program, and the other a change specialist, a consultant. It's worth a try. The important thing is to focus the change session on your supervisors. If you can sell them on it, you've got it made."

Marty was listening to Sylvie, but he was also thinking about the Supervisors in his detachment. Even if he could sell the idea to HQ, he still had some hard cases among the Supervisors.

"But what's the change part going to be about? If it's too general, people will just tune out. A lot of us have been so disappointed in the past that we're not that open to change."

Sylvie was nodding in agreement. "That's just the reason for addressing change. Over the years a lot of resistance can be built up when planned changes don't materialize. People become cynical. You've already told us that this software program is going to be one of the biggest changes of all. Maybe, just because of that, there will be a lot of resistance to it. Think about it. We're all paid to do our jobs because of the way things are now. Bureaucracy legitimizes resistance. With something new, all of that changes. All of a sudden we're asked to do something that goes against what our jobs have been all about. That means resistance at some level, and people need to know about what they can be expected to go through."

"Yeah, I hear you, but I've also been told in no uncertain terms that we're not to 'mollycoddle' people. They either get with the program, or get out. A lot of people who should know better don't see change as an issue." Marty shook his head at his memory of the conversation with Steve Harwood, his contact for the new initiative.

"Maybe you've got to try harder to make your point," Sylvie countered. "I mean you're the one on the front line. You know what you're up against. Start with that. Zero in on why you need to address change at the Supervisory level before you get into describing the new computer program. It's worth a try if you feel it's important."

Marty looked sharply at Sylvie, as if he had just heard something very important that he had forgotten about. He smiled. "I think it's very, very important, and I will do something about it."

At the Office

Over the next week, Marty reviewed reports on other changes that had taken place within the police force, and he took the time to talk to his people about what concerned them. At first they seemed a little surprised that someone was actually asking their opinion. It seemed a novelty to them. Armed with a great deal of direct, front line information, he made an appointment to see Steve Harwood at Headquarters.

"So you're telling me you think we need some scum-sucking consultant come in here to tell us what we already know we need?"

"Not quite. I want this training to work, and I know you do too. To do it right, we need to get the Supervisors on side. If they want it to happen, it will," Marty said.

"I'm suggesting we focus on a session with them first, before we start training all staff. The session I have in mind won't focus on the new software. It'll deal with change and some of the benefits of the new system, and that's where the consultant comes in."

"I'm hearing you Marty, but I still don't see where the consultant fits in."

"The consultant will be there to talk about change in general, to set the stage for the change in thinking that the new software will bring with it."

Steve Harwood observed Marty closely. "All right, I'm willing to bring someone in, but I want you to work with the consultant closely. As a matter of fact, I want it to be a team approach. I want you to be a key part of it. That way we can stay focused on what needs to be done. Agreed?"

Marty smiled. "That's O.K. with me."

"In the meantime," Steve continued, " I'll find out who's the best consultant to work with on the change issue. We have enough of them around. Not all of them are scum-suckers. We have to get the right fit, or it won't work. You have a lot of credibility with the force. The consultant we choose has to have the same credibility, and just as importantly, the right fit. I'll get back to you in a few days. What about a coffee?"

"That would be great," Marty said.

Over the next few days Marty thought about the new software. He spoke to the developers of the program and to some of the trainers. He needed to know why it was needed. Unless he could readily see the reason behind adopting it, how could he be expected to endorse it? He wanted to get at some clear and tangible benefits. Nothing else would do. He knew his staff. They were practical people. They needed to see how they could use it, and how it was more effective than what they had now. He went up to the whiteboard on the conference room wall and drew a large T with a heavy black marker. Above the T, he wrote **What's Happening Now** on the top left-hand side, and **What Should Be Happening** on the top right-hand side of the T.

He started jotting down points on the left side of the chart. He focused on the things that were happening now that he knew he and his staff didn't like. Things like not being able to read reports because of poor handwriting, and lost files, and duplication. Marty knew that many organizations faced the same problems with information management, but that didn't make it any easier to accept. The situation needed to change. It took him less than ten minutes to outline both sides of the chart. The right-hand side was easy enough. It was just the opposite of the problem listed on the left-hand side of the chart. It made sense to him, and if it worked for him, it would work for others.

The following Tuesday, Marty met with the consultant that HQ had selected to deliver the change component of the training. The consultant, Jim Randall, was a tall, slim man with a ready smile and an engaging manner. Marty knew it was important to address change in a general sense, but he had some reservations about how it would be received. His staffers were a practical, focused group. They wouldn't look too kindly on a lecture on why change was needed. They'd been through that before.

Marty spent his first hour with the consultant reviewing what he knew about the new program and how it differed from the manual methods they used currently. They sat opposite one another at a small table in the Tim Horton's Coffee Shop across from the police station. Marty showed him the T-Chart reinforcing the before and after shots of the situation. He emphasized how crucial it was to focus on elements of the program his staffers could use right away. Jim Randall listened attentively and nodded. He waited patiently until Marty had covered everything he thought he should know. Marty liked the fact that Jim was taking notes as he spoke.

"Jim, how do you plan to talk about change when we meet with the supervisory group?"

"The first thing I aim to do is to ask them what they expect from our session together. I know they'll have already received a brief blurb telling them about the new program, but it's important for us to gauge what they think about the change initiative from the very outset. Some of them are bound to be a bit frustrated with still another change coming their way. You've already told me that we can expect some reservations. I want to find out where they're at."

"Jim, I'm just glad you're doing the generic change part. I wouldn't want to be doing it. We're going to hit a few rough spots, I'm sure of that."

"The rough spots are the resistance to change. That's natural. I want to open discussion on just the kinds of resistance they feel themselves, and that they anticipate the people under them will feel too."

"What do mean by resistance," Marty asked.

"The experts say that there are four phases involved. These phases include denial, resistance, exploration, and commitment. The phases don't move smoothly from one to another, but there are things to look for in each phase."

"Like what?"

"The first two, denial and resistance are the dangerous parts. For instance, let's look at denial. What you notice in this phase are things like a lack of caring, a kind of numbness and feeling that the change will pass. There's usually some fear or apprehension about the change. In the active resistance stage, you can expect more anxiety especially when the new system breaks down. What you see in this phase are people opting out, maybe greater absenteeism and less trust. There's often some sort of conflict between people about the changed roles they're experiencing. It's not that people are actively sabotaging the change so much that they're afraid of it. After all, the systems that are in place, the old systems, are what they serve, and these systems have to do with the work they're paid to do."

"Are there ways to lessen the resistance somehow, to make it go down easier?"

"The best way," Jim said, "is to communicate, to talk about why the change is happening, and to make the purpose crystal clear. Your people need to be involved and feel they have a stake in things. They need to see the benefits in adopting the new system, and they need to believe in it."

"How are we going to do that?"

"We have to communicate what we intend to do in the way we talk to them about the workshop and what's going to happen. The e-mails that we send out have to spell it out. We have to invite them to participate in what we're going to do. We have to secure their involvement. If we don't do that, we're bound to meet with resistance. Communication is essential so that we can dispel any fears they may have."

"Even if they've been told that they're expected to commit to the new program," Marty said.

"Especially then. The old days of 'command and control' are over. You've told me that already."

"O.K., now what about the other two phases or stages you mentioned. What are they?"

"As I said, the phases aren't that neat. There's always some degree of transition between each phase. After the resistance phase, we get into exploration. People will be exploring what the program can do and may feel a bit overwhelmed by it all. At first they'll be expending a lot of energy on the program, but they may lack focus. There's bound to be frustration during this phase until the last stage of commitment is reached. But when it is reached, they will feel satisfaction because they'll be experiencing the benefits. That's when real teamwork will kick in."

A few weeks later they were ready. They had rehearsed their presentation, and they felt comfortable with it. All of the police supervisors had been contacted and had been sent e-mails outlining the contents of the workshop. Essentially, the half-day presentation would present ideas on change followed by an overview of the new information management program and its benefits. Actual training for the supervisors on the new program would come later. It was simple and focused. Despite all of their preparations, Marty still felt some qualms. On the morning of their pilot presentation, before the supervisors had arrived, Jim asked Marty how he was feeling.

"A little nervous Jim, just a little." Marty was moving desks and chairs to structure a U-formation for the workshop participants. Jim was assisting him as he spoke.

"You know, I can feel it too. There's a little anxiety in the pit of my stomach. Right here."

"But you've done this hundreds of times. It's your job." Marty stopped for a moment and looked at Jim with surprise.

"Yes, I have, but not to this next group, here, today. If I didn't feel a little anxious, I'd be worried. In my business you can't afford to grow complacent. The anxiety gives you an edge that you can use."

Soon, the supervisors began arriving and taking their seats behind the name-cards that Jim had prepared. Marty observed how Jim approached each Supervisor and introduced himself. Jim nodded to Marty to begin the session. Marty cleared his throat gruffly and began. He remembered the tips on giving a presentation that he had learned from his supervisory friends over lunch.

"We'd like to start with your expectations of the session. All of you have received the e-mails we sent describing the change in recording information with the new program, but we want to know what you want from our time together today. I'll note them in point form on the flipchart here so we keep them in mind as we're making our presentations."

A burly corporal a few seats away from Marty coughed. "Well, for one thing, I'd like to know what it's all about. I didn't get any information about it. All I know is that I'm losing a half day that I could spend doing some real police work."

"You didn't get our e-mail?"

"Nope. I don't know about that. I was told to report here this morning when I came into the office."

A sergeant sitting next to Marty shook his head and guffawed. "Did you bother to open your e-mail? I made sure I passed the information on to everyone a week ago."

"Maybe I didn't. I went through all my regular mail though, the paper mail," the corporal said, squirming in his seat.

"A lot of us aren't used to working the computer," a constable said.

"Marty, it might be useful to go over the memo we sent out," Jim Randall offered.

Marty took a few moments to communicate the change initiative and to address the purpose and rationale of the change session. He used a T-chart to elicit their responses on what they were doing now with their paper reporting, and then he filled in what the new program would do, stressing the benefits of electronic reporting over paper reporting. "So that's it," Marty said, by way of conclusion, "No more lost files, no more needless duplication. The transfer of files will be instantaneous. The information will be at your fingertips, and your reports will be a lot easier to generate."

Jim followed Marty's introduction with an overview of the session, what would happen when according to the agenda, and then presented his change model. He moved easily between the whiteboard and screen using a laser pointer to emphasize and draw attention to his key points. He had almost finished when a clearly exasperated sergeant interrupted him.

"You keep talking about resistance. We don't have any resistance. There's no resistance here. Marty has already told us that the top brass wants to go in this direction. So why do you keep harping on resistance. It's not an issue."

"It may or may not be," Jim replied. He could hear the rising anger in the sergeant's voice. "The important thing is to be aware of it. As supervisors, you may feel that resistance is a non-issue, but that may not be the case with all of your subordinates. Remember, neither you nor your subordinates have had training on the new information system. Old ways of doing things are sometimes difficult to give up. You may encounter resistance in some of your people. It's natural. You have to be prepared for that."

"Well what kind of resistance? My people are law officers. They're not going to sabotage something that will make their jobs easier to do. I don't get this resistance thing. They're not the bad guys."

Jim nodded. "Of course not. Resistance comes in different forms. If some of your people haven't touched a computer before, they're apt to be a little reluctant to do so now, with the new program. It's a big shift in thinking from paper reporting to electronic reporting. Not everyone learns at the same rate. They're going to need your help, as supervisors, as coaches. That's the reason for this session, to give you a heads-up on what to expect. Now, I've been talking about change, but soon, Marty will give you an overview of the new program. You won't be trained on the new program today. We just want to outline to you what it can do."

"O.K.," the sergeant said, "let's see it."

Marty gave a 20-minute overview covering the features of the program. While he was going through the demonstration, he observed the growing interest amongst the group. They became animated and talkative. They could readily see the benefits. Time spent in preparing reports would be drastically reduced. They talked informally until the group was dismissed for a coffee break. Marty was stirring a second packet of sugar into his coffee when the sergeant approached him.

"Marty, I'm not the most computer-savvy guy in the detachment. How am I going to be able to help someone if they run into a problem. Do you know what I mean?"

Marty sipped at his coffee. "That's where the coaching comes in. Some of your staff will be learning at a faster rate than others. A few are going to advance quickly. You can pair up people to make sure the learning sticks. If someone needs extra help, you can have the trainers come back for a refresher course. The important thing is for you to support your team until it gets up to speed. And remember, Jim and I are here to help with any situations that you encounter. Here's my contact number."

After the break, Marty and Jim outlined strategies that the supervisors could use to manage and support the change effort. They addressed ways to anticipate and plan change through communication, training, and follow-up. There were common-sense strategies aimed at reinforcing positive acceptance of the new program. Jim also talked about "celebrating change."

"Once people are using the new system, celebrate it. Take a half-hour out of your week to let people know the benefits that utilization of the new software is bringing to their work. That's important. It might even be better to order a few pizzas to go along with it. It's important to ask people how things are going and to do it informally. Follow-up is essential. You can't take anything for granted. Talk to your people. "

After the workshop Marty and Jim took their lunch and reviewed what they had done. Marty was a little disappointed over the reaction to the segment on change.

"It's what I expected," Jim said. "There's always bound to be some denial and resistance even if people say there isn't. It comes with the territory. The important thing is to accept it and allow some venting to take place. We have to go through those phases to get at the later stages of exploration, actually trying out the new program, until we get commitment to it. It's a process, and it's necessary."

"I guess so, but it's tough."

"Sure is, but it's a useful model to show them because they're going to experience it firsthand when their people begin using the new program. I've learned through hard experience that a conceptual model helps people to understand what's going on. Behind any successful change initiative there has to be a clear purpose, a useful process to clarify what's needed, and committed people. That's what we began accomplishing today with this change workshop. Now, we have to do our best on reinforcing the change to electronic reporting. We have to make sure the supervisors have the resources they need to support their people. We also have to follow-up on the training to make certain it's been effective."

Marty smiled. "We need to continue to communicate. I think we're on the right track."

"We'll get there. It just takes a bit of patience, some understanding, and a little time." Jim held up his coffee cup signaling to the waitress to bring more coffee.

Inukshuk Four : Manage Change

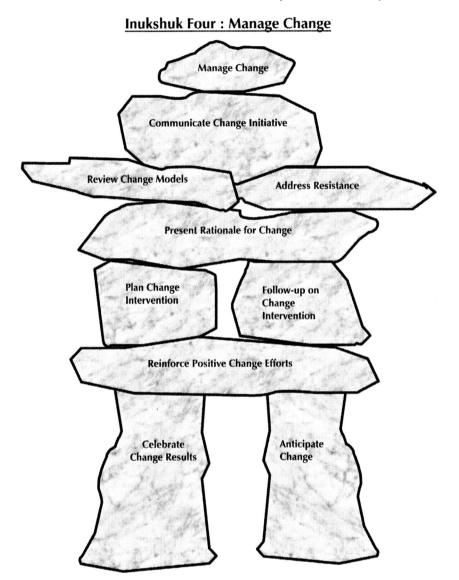

Super Skill: Optimize Teams

Profile Five: Sylvie Morriseau

Sylvie Morriseau is an experienced Supervisor who is using a team-based approach to examine processes on the plant floor. Her problem is to utilize her team without abandoning all of her authority to make decisions. She encourages consensus building within her teams but that has resulted in the team feeling that she does not act on their input and recommendations. A few have told her that she has conned them into believing that all of them would make decisions together; however, some of them contend she has arbitrarily made decisions that were not agreed to by all team members. She realizes that she needs to get them on side in order to examine the many work processes that operate on the floor.

At the Plant

Sylvie had some serious doubts regarding the new work assignment she was given. Two words summed it all up: continuous improvement. Twenty per cent of her supervisory time was to be devoted to improving work processes within the plant. She was free to do whatever she wished to accomplish that goal. Senior management had told her that the many small improvements that she had championed over the years had made her a clear favorite for what they termed "an enhanced supervisory role." Their praise was accompanied by a financial incentive that was pegged to quality and productivity improvements.

After the initial euphoria had worn off, she had sat down on her office chair with a thud, unlike her. Sylvie was a lithe, sprightly woman who attacked challenges head-on, but this situation was different. Where do you begin to "continuously improve?" What area of operations do you choose? Who do you consult with? When do you start? Why? So many questions raced within her. She stared up at the ceiling and felt a wave of panic flood over her. She didn't like feeling rudderless and doubtful. She needed to find a place to start, so instinctively she left her office and went for a walk on the plant floor.

Thursday Dim Sum

"What's the most difficult part about this process thing?" Gary asked while pouring some tea into Sylvie's cup. Around their table, the other three supervisors were engaged in conversation as well. The restaurant was busy and buzzing with that special noise that develops when people are enjoying themselves and talking over a fine meal.

Sylvie smiled. "You won't believe it, but it's the team. Let me explain what I mean. We've got small teams in control of each of the key processes in the plant. The teams have to work together, and with me, to make it work. It's the way we work together that's so important, how we communicate and interact with each other. The trouble is, some of my people think they know better than the team. The funny thing is, they're my star performers. They're exceptional. I don't know quite how to put it. My best people sometimes interfere with the team, and how we make decisions together. They're impatient, I guess. They want improvements to happen too fast, before everyone on the team understands why or how."

"Wait a minute," Gary said, "you mean to tell me that you're holding up improvements to your processes because some people on your team don't understand why you're making the change?"

"Yup," Sylvie said, sipping at her jasmine tea.

"I don't understand what you mean," Gary said.

Sylvie looked thoughtfully at her tea for a moment and then back at Gary. "I don't know as much as I'd like to about people, but I do know that when people join a team, certain issues come up again and again."

"Like who's in control?"

" That's part of it. I'm thinking more about basic issues, personal questions that people ask of themselves. Gary, it's not so different from the time we were all kids in the schoolyard. What I'm trying to say is that the first question everyone asks when they join a team is a simple, very human one. Am I 'in' or 'out?' You know the feeling. We all do. Everyone wants to feel a real part of things. Do you know what I mean?"

"Yeah, it's not something that's talked about a lot, but I think I know what you mean. Look at me. Part of my biggest problem is getting my manager to accept me on the team. When I first started working as a supervisor, I know I was on the outside. That's what was so confusing. I've always thought of supervisors as being part of management."

"And they are," Sylvie agreed. "They're on the front lines. Sometimes, they're forgotten. I mean, we're forgotten."

"Tell me about it. I know exactly what you mean. That's been one of the biggest problems I've faced- not feeling that I'm a part of the management team, not feeling 'in.'"

Sylvie nodded. "And along with that, there are the other questions. 'Do I have any power and control?' Everybody likes to feel that they have some control. I'm not talking about lording it over somebody. What I mean is the feeling that you have some influence, that, as a supervisor, you're actually listened to, that you have some value. "

"Right on. That's what I'm after," Gary said.

Frank Buchar

"And that," Sylvie continued, "brings us to the third question. 'Can you grow and develop your skills as a contributing member of the team?' It's kind of like pride of craftsmanship. Do you know what I mean?"

"I know exactly what you mean."

Sylvie looked around the table and suddenly grew very intense and serious.

"These questions, if they're answered positively, set the conditions, the right conditions for individuals to feel right about their place on a team. Just that, nothing more. Everyone wants to feel good about themselves. I think it's up to the team leader or supervisor to set the right conditions. That means a lot of openness, a lot of feedback, good and bad. If you want to get the best out of your people, out of your teams, you have to think long and hard about what you can do to make people feel comfortable about their place on the team, any team. The funny thing is that most teams almost always focus on their work, on the tasks in front of them and leave the people issues behind. You can't do that and expect a team to thrive. People are human, and they need the right kind of attention." Sylvie was suddenly aware of the quietness around the table.

"Sorry everyone," Sylvie said, "I guess that sounded like a sermon. I didn't mean that. Sorry."

"If that's a sermon, tell us more," Raymond said. "You're right. Too often the human part of a team gets lost in the shuffle. Everybody's so fixated on doing their job, they forget that part, the human part. Without that, things on a team can go wrong, very wrong."

"You know," Marty said, " What I'm hearing when Sylvie's talking about these team questions is something a lot like what I'm facing with change. These team conditions are the kinds of issues I'm faced with in this change initiative. People want to feel that they've been considered in the equation, that their input is valued. What it says to me is that these supervisory skills aren't all separate and self-contained. These skills aren't in little compartments that you take out one at a time. They're not like that at all. They dovetail into one another, and as soon

76

as you pick up one, you pick up another too. Building a team is a lot like setting the right conditions for change."

"And that takes us back to the inukshuk concept," Raymond said. "Each of the stones on a specific supervisory inukshuk, say teambuilding, is interchangeable with another, like change, as Marty has already pointed out. The thing to remember is that as a Supervisor you have a full range of supervisory skills at your fingertips. The kinds of competencies you display when you're strengthening a team is also applicable to advancing a change initiative. That's the beauty of it. It's all there ready for you to use once you've mastered the fundamentals of supervision. Once you've done that, you can give direction, like an inukshuk."

At the Plant

Sylvie listened patiently to Ransom Myers as he detailed the kinds of changes he wanted to implement in his work section. Ransom was a formal, young man, slightly balding, who carried about thirty extra pounds, most of it concentrated around his mid-section. The trouble, she thought, as Ransom droned on, was his condescending attitude. She glanced around the table at the team of nine, and noticed a few team members rolling their eyeballs. Ransom was brilliant, but distanced himself from everyone. He just didn't think anyone had any worthwhile ideas. It showed in his poor listening skills. He never heard anyone out. He was always interrupting, stating his point of view before anyone had a chance to finish theirs. And now, as he presented his last PowerPoint slide, he sat on the edge of the heavy board room table, and said, "Any questions?"

"What input have you had from people on the floor?" Tina Hartling asked. Sylvie appreciated Tina's comments at team meetings. She always thought about the stakeholders who were not there, the people who would be directly affected by her team's decisions.

"None," Ransom said. "I didn't need input. I've analyzed the situation from every possible angle. My proposal is the best possible solution. I've just shifted a few responsibilities, that's all."

"But you can't do that," Tina said.

"What do you mean I can't do that? That's what this team is all about, to make changes that improve workflow. That's our mandate. This is about ideas that work, not about whether the staff like it or not. Personal preferences are not part of the equation."

Tina glanced across the table at Sylvie, looking for support. "What I'm trying to point out is that the union won't allow us to arbitrarily change job responsibilities like that."

"I think Tina has a point. We need to get input from the floor. If we impose our thinking on them, the changes that we're making won't take hold. We've gone that route before. We need their full support. Any suggestions on how we can secure their involvement?"

Ransom smirked. "You know, asking for input is one thing, getting it is another. A few months ago we installed a suggestion box on the floor. Has anyone seen any serious ideas come from that box? I sure haven't. That was a lot of wasted effort."

Tina cleared her throat. "There again, I don't think we made enough of an effort. We posted a notice on the bulletin board and left it at that. I mean, hindsight builds monuments. We learned something from that. We should have talked to people directly about what the suggestion box was all about. We can't leave it as a kind of osmosis and just expect things to happen."

Sylvie nodded in agreement. "I agree. Let's meet with them at shift change next Tuesday for half an hour. We can present the changes and ask for their input then. I'll talk to the supervisors and make sure the extra time is covered. O.K.?"

Ransom shifted his bulk uneasily on the boardroom table. "Why not?" he said sarcastically. "You're the boss on the team. You're going to do what you want to do anyway. That's team leadership, isn't it?"

Sylvie felt a surge of anger rush through her chest. She felt constricted, compressed, ready to explode. Everyone's eyes were on her, waiting, expectant. For a moment she said nothing, summoning control from deep within herself, breathing quietly and deeply. When she was ready, Sylvie said slowly, "I don't think that's fair. The purpose of this team is make improvements to work processes. We do that together. It's important that we all agree on what we plan to do. That includes other stakeholders not here at this meeting, people who are going to be directly affected. I am the team leader, as you point out, and as team leader, I have certain responsibilities, but I do not arbitrarily make decisions that this team disagrees with."

Ransom cleared his throat and stared at the ceiling tiles. Tina, recognizing the impasse, broke the growing silence by suggesting an adjournment. "Look we've covered as much as we can today. Let's meet again next week, same time. By then we'll have had input from the others, and we can decide on an action plan. What do you say?"

The motion was quietly seconded, and everyone quickly left the meeting room, leaving Tina and Sylvie behind. Sylvie sighed and smiled wryly at Tina. "Well I guess the team is going through some growing pains. I thought that we were making sure everyone felt a part of things and could contribute freely. I sure didn't see that coming. Ransom seems to have a few issues with my leadership."

"Ransom has issues with everyone's leadership except his own," Tina offered.

"Still," Sylvie said, "we have to address that, or we're not going to be able to meet our goals. The question is how?"

Tina shrugged and shook her head.

Thursday Dim Sum

"Sylvie," Marty said, "it's the team process that needs to be discussed and defined, how people are communicating, and how they're getting along. I know you've always been sensitive to it, but it sounds like you really need to articulate it. Your team needs guidelines on how they want to interact."

"You mean something written down, like a contract?"

"Yes. You can call it that if you like. Your team needs to come up with how they're going to communicate with each other. A few egos are probably going to be bruised, but it needs to be done. The team can decide what it won't put up with in the way people talk to each other. They'll also decide on how decisions are going to be made. Have you thought about that?"

"Well I told them we'd make decisions together, by consensus."

"But what does that mean?" Marty queried. "What happens if someone disagrees, like Ransom Myers?"

Sylvie looked puzzled. "I haven't really wrestled with the mechanics of it. I guess my idea of consensus was a majority vote."

Marty leaned forward as if to emphasize his next question. "So, you're willing to give up control and final decision-making on any issue, if the majority of the team votes against a decision you want to make?"

Sylvie smiled, as if she had been checkmated in a chess game. "Well no, not on every issue. It depends on the situation of course. I'm sure there will be times when I want input from people, and perhaps their recommendations on a course of action, but after all is said and done, I'll make the final decision."

"Good. Meet with your team and ask them to develop guidelines with you on how the team wants to communicate, and on how they will share decision-making responsibilities with you. Tell them up front that decision-making responsibilities will change depending on what's on the table."

The dim sum cart stopped in front of their table. "Raymond, let's order some more of those delicious shrimp dumplings. What are they called in Cantonese?"

"They're called *har kow*," he said. "Let's also try some of the steamed beef balls and spring rolls. Just the thing to accompany a discussion on teams."

At the Plant

Sylvie drew a huge T on the whiteboard in the team meeting room. "I want to focus our attention on how the team is meeting, on process issues." Above the top left side of the letter T she wrote: **What's Happening Now;** on the right hand side, she wrote: **What Should Be Happening.** "We've been at cross purposes during too many of our team meetings and I want it to change for the better. So let's start here. Tell me what you think is messing up how we meet. The floor is yours."

Tina raised her hand tentatively, summoning up the courage to address something that had been bothering her for a long time. "Some people monopolize time. They take over, and not everyone has a chance to contribute."

There was a long silence after Tina's remark. It was as if the others around the table sensed an opportunity for change. They didn't hesitate to take it.

"The meetings always run overtime. They're too long."

"There's too much bad blood between some people. You can feel the tension in the air. How can you make positive recommendations with all that negativity around?"

"My biggest beef is with the decision-making process. If we're a team, why doesn't the team decide what needs to be done? Sometimes I think these team meetings are just a screen for something that's being decided privately, or that's already been decided. It's just so hypocritical. Who needs it?"

"I don't really think that what I have to say, my input at these meetings, is valued. Because of that, I feel that my time is being wasted when I could be actually doing some work."

"We always seem to get off topic. Our meetings are so rambling. They go everywhere and get nowhere."

"People seem bored."

"Nothing seems to happen as a result of these meetings. There's no follow up, so far as I can see."

"The biggest thing for me is how we talk to each other. It's terrible. It's sunk to a new low."

"The whole idea of team consensus, and making decisions based on mutual agreement is a crock. Regardless of what the team says, you decide what you want to do anyway."

Sylvie had been writing down their comments with a red felt tip marker, in point form, on the whiteboard. The left side of the T chart, **What's Happening Now**, was startling to her as she stood away from it for a moment. "O.K.," Sylvie said, "I think we've got something to work with. Have I captured all of the ideas? Do you want any changes made?"

Sylvie looked at her team. There were murmurs of agreement and a few nods. She smiled, a little ruefully. "I had no idea it was this bad."

"You never asked," Ransom Myers said flatly.

Sylvie, ignoring Ransom's cutting remark, moved quickly to the right side of the whiteboard and selected a green felt tip marker to replace the red one she had been using. "It's time for change. You've shared what's not working as far as the team is concerned. Now, here and now, I want your suggestions for improvement. Who'll start?"

"Do you really think this exercise will do any good?" Ransom said sarcastically.

Tina glared across the table at him. "It's worth a try," she said. "Sylvie's trying to get us on the right track while you seem to be doing everything you can to hold things back. It's what you do at all of our meetings. I'd just like to know why."

"I've told you. The whole team decision-making thing is a lie. It's not what we decide. It's what Sylvie decides. Think about it. Every time we meet and decide on something, the results that we see on the plant floor are different from the decisions we made. Tell me I'm wrong."

Sylvie tightened her grip on the felt tip marker she held in her hands. She considered how to respond. She knew she had worked three times as hard as any male to reach the supervisory position she held. The managers she reported to had never made any concessions for women rising through the ranks. Even some of her subordinates, including bright, ambitious engineers such as Ransom Myers, had undermined her authority from the beginning. She was not about to buckle under any rancid criticism that had no basis in fact. Sylvie leveled her gaze at Ransom.

"You're obviously very angry about our decision-making process. That's clear to everyone, especially me. That's what we need to focus on. I can promise you that we'll address that, and all of the issues listed here. But first, in order to deal with these issues, we have to agree on how we'll talk to each other, on how we'll communicate. I don't respond very well to angry, emotional outbursts. I don't think anyone on the team does. Am I correct?"

There was an awkward silence that was followed by one or two comments signaling agreement. Ransom rolled his eyes and turned his head away from Sylvie with a smirk.

"That's just what I mean Ransom," Sylvie said coolly. "You're not treating this problem that we have seriously. I'm talking about how we communicate. For one thing, I resent the lack of respect you're showing to me right now with your body language. We have to begin by establishing some formal guidelines on how we'll talk to each other. All of us."

"You're the boss," Ransom said, crossing his arms and settling deep into his seat.

Sylvie was momentarily flustered, but concealed it by printing on the white board. When she turned to face the group, she was in control again, and determined. "So, we have our first point: develop communication guidelines. I'd like to suggest that we spell out what we mean. Who wants to start us off?"

"I will," Tina said. "Our team meetings will not tolerate disrespectful or abusive talk or behavior."

"Good," Sylvie said, taking down the point made on the white board. Other comments began almost at once, as the group warmed to their task. Sylvie worked quickly to capture the ideas in point form.

"Team members will not interrupt others while they are speaking."

"Everyone will have an opportunity to express their ideas."

"Each team member will be allowed an equal amount of talk time."

"Silence on any issue before the group will be taken to mean agreement."

"Good," Sylvie said. "Is everyone comfortable with this? Anything to add?" Sylvie noticed that Ransom squirmed slightly in his seat. "We should have tackled this issue when we first started meeting, but better late than never. Keep in mind that we can always add to these guidelines if we need to. The important thing is that we all agree to abide by them. I'll include them in the meeting minutes."

"What about decision-making?" Ransom asked, sitting up in his seat.

"Sure," Sylvie said. 'Where do you want to start?"

"I'd just like to see some clear guidelines on decision-making that we can all accept. What's really bothered me is that a lot of decisions that were made here, by this team, never made it to the floor. Can you help us with that?"

"I think I can, and I'm sorry that I haven't been clear on that issue. It's caused a lot of misunderstandings, and that's my fault as team leader." Sylvie sat down and looked around at the group. Everyone, including Ransom, was listening intently.

"First things first," she said, using her hands to push away a file folder in front of her. "I want you to know that all of the decisions and recommendations we make here have to go through our management group. That's a given. They can decide to veto any decision we make, regardless of the team's consensus. That's one of the reasons why we don't always see the changes we've recommended on the floor. Like it or not, that's the way it is, and I want you to know that.

I should have made that crystal clear from the beginning. I'm sorry I didn't."

"But they haven't vetoed all of the recommendations we've made, have they?" Ransom asked.

"No, they haven't. There have been times when I asked for your input and then made the decision I thought was best. I should have been more explicit."

"So, when do we know if the management group, or you, or the team, is going to make the final decision?"

"I'll let you know about the responsibility for decision-making before we begin discussion on an issue. I can promise you that. But I need your help. Are you willing to work with me on this until we get it right?" Sylvie tilted her head to one side and waited for a reply. She didn't know whether she would receive agreement to her proposed course of action or an insult. She was prepared for either.

Ransom smiled. "You only had to ask."

Tina glanced quickly at Sylvie to see her reaction. For a moment, her expression, especially around her eyes, was one of critical assessment, and then Sylvie's dimpled smile engaged them all in a common bond. The group erupted into peals of laughter for the first, but not the last time.

Frank Buchar

Inukshuk Five : Optimize Teams

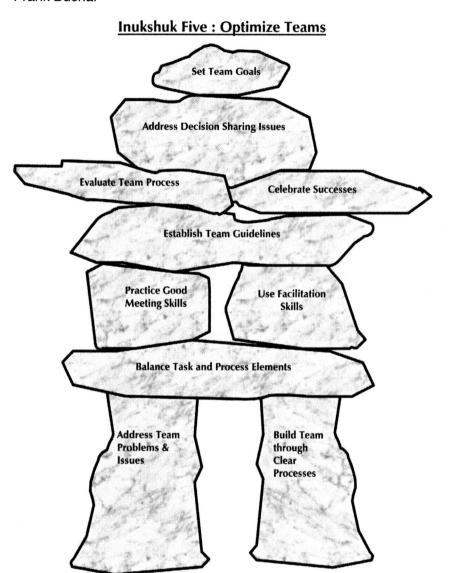

Super Skill: Motivate Staff and Maintain Discipline

Profile Six: Gary Clark

As Gary gains expertise in supervising staff, he encounters some staff who wish to manipulate him for their own ends and others who give freely of their skills and talent. Given input from experienced supervisors, he learns to apply thorough and objective approaches in dealing with situations that require both motivation and discipline.

Thursday Dim Sum

"Different things motivate different people. There's no one generic brand that satisfies everyone. You can't get into someone's head and 'motivate' them. Even an expensive brain surgeon can't do that. But there are ways to motivate, " Raymond said in response to Gary's query about motivation.

"Sure," Sylvie quipped, her short, silky brown hair shining as she spoke. "All of the ways can be folded neatly into a wallet. It's called money."

"That'll work for a while, but it doesn't last," Raymond countered. "Think about it. Those abandoned Christmas presents that are lying around the house in March don't have the same allure as they did when they were all wrapped up on

Christmas Eve. People adjust to a raise pretty quickly. Maybe it's human nature, I don't know, but they always seem to want more. That's the whole basis of modern advertising."

"So you've got me hooked. What are the other ways? I sure could use a primer on motivation." Gary poured everyone a fresh cup of tea.

"You'll probably laugh when I say this, but I think you have to be a lot like Sherlock Holmes."

"I never thought of him as a Supervisor, Raymond," Sylvie said, her eyes smiling.

"Don't you remember Watson? Sherlock was always coaching him, motivating him. What I'm trying to point out is that you have to observe people over time to see what motivates them. Just think about your own family. Everybody's different."

"That may be," Sylvie said, "but I sure don't have the budget to play Santa Claus."

"I maintain that money doesn't have staying power as a motivator. It fades quickly." Raymond sipped at his tea.

""So what can we do?" Gary asked.

"Observe. Listen. Do something. Think about the person you want to motivate. Watch them. Listen to them. When you think you know what motivates them, act on it. It may be that they want more time off, or recognition, or just a polite thank you. Once you recognize what it is, act on it. Say something, or do something. You have to reward good behaviour."

"But what if you want someone to be motivated enough just to do their job. I mean some people just don't do enough," Gary said. "To me, they're already being rewarded by being paid."

"Every situation is different, and everyone's unique. If someone isn't performing well, and you want to motivate them, focus on the things they're doing well. Reward that. That's the lever to use. Don't focus on their weakness. Minimize it. A few years ago, at my plant, we had a brilliant research engineer who was probably the most creative, productive man I've ever met. This guy was brilliant, but he was a sloppy dresser. The management we had at that time had a strict dress code, and they insisted everyone conform to it. This engineer just wouldn't conform, and so he left. We were never able to replace the skills he brought to our team, though his replacements were all impeccably dressed. It's an odd story, but true. Do what you can in little ways to strengthen the weakness, but your emphasis should be on their strengths. I mean, think about it. The worst thing you can do to motivate somebody to do something better is by yelling and screaming at them. I've tried that routine. It never worked."

"It didn't work for me either," Sylvie said. "What you're saying is worth a try. Screaming doesn't work. It's just finding out what makes people tick that's the hard part."

Raymond leaned back in his chair. "Did you ever hear about Maslow, Abraham Maslow? He was a thinker about what motivates people, and he came up with what he called a 'pyramid of needs.'"

"Is it like an inukshuk?" Terry asked.

"Kinda." Raymond spread out his napkin and drew a rough triangle on it. He then drew four horizontal lines within it, dividing it into five distinct areas.

"O.K., here's the pyramid. At the base of it are basic needs like food and shelter. The next level is basic security and safety. It's about freedom from fear, and having a stable environment. This third area here," he said, using his pencil tip to point it out, "is social acceptance, having friends and human contact with others. From there we move into self-esteem needs. This area is about feeling important, that you have something to offer, that you're valued and needed. And here, at the apex of the triangle, you have what Maslow called the 'self-actualized' person. This is a person doing exactly what he wants and needs to do. This is the peak of being motivated. You see, as we move from one level to another, it's important to remember that you can't motivate a person through their higher needs until the more basic needs are met. A man's not going to be concerned about reaching his true work potential if he's hungry. He'll be thinking about food, a need that's basic to his survival. Once that's satisfied, he can move on to these higher needs. Make sense?"

"Yeah, it does," Gary said, looking at the napkin. "Money isn't the motivator. But what about good old-fashioned fear as an incentive? I've noticed that when my manager walks the floor everyone seems to buck up and move a little faster. Do you know what I mean?"

"I know exactly what you mean. That's the big stick approach. Fear as an incentive doesn't last long. It makes people defensive, and when they feel intimidated or threatened, they can't be motivated in a positive, sustained way. You can't function, here, in this self-actualized area," Raymond emphasized, shading in the top of the pyramid with his pencil, " if you're afraid."

At the Plant

Tommy Johnson sauntered into Gary's office and sat in the chair opposite Gary's desk. "Hi bro, so tell me, how'd you like the fish?" Gary looked up from the production report he was reviewing and saw Johnson's broad smiling face. "Oh, I haven't had it yet. It's huge. I'm waiting until I have some company over before I cook it up."

"Gary, there's something I'd like to ask you. My cousin's getting married next week, and I wanted a few days off. The thing is, I don't have any holiday time left. I can cover one of the days with the overtime I've got left, but that leaves two days that I need. Can you help me out?"

"Why don't you see if someone will cover for you?"

"Already have. Everybody's tied up."

"Sorry Tommy. If no one's available, you're it."

"Aw, c'mon bro. Just this once."

"Can't do it."

"Fine," Johnson said, and then turned, abruptly leaving the office. He slammed the door behind him. Gary shook his head and returned to his review of the production report.

A week later Gary listened to his voice mail. "Good morning Gary. It's Tommy Johnson. I won't be able to make it in. I'm not feeling very good. I think it's one of my allergies again. My doctor told me to stay put for a while. Hope you can find someone to fill my slot. Bye."

Gary smiled wryly as he listened to Johnson. It seemed highly coincidental to him that his allergies flared up just when he needed some extra time off. He raced to the floor to see if someone would cover an extra shift.

The following week Gary had arranged to have a meeting with Tommy Johnson. Gary glanced at his watch. Johnson was ten minutes late. He brushed back a hank of hair from across his forehead and waited. His cup of coffee cooled in front of him. He hated situations like this. What can you do, he thought, when you have suspicions about a subordinate abusing the system and can't prove it? He believed that Tommy Johnson had called in sick to cover the time he wanted off. But proving it was another matter. Johnson entered his office, smiling.

"Hi, bro. You wanted to see me?" Johnson sat down in the chair in front of Gary's desk.

"Yeah Tommy. I wanted to talk to you about last week. You were off two days."

"I called in. I left a message for you. Some of my allergies were acting up again. I hear Vinko filled in for me and worked a double shift. He did O.K. for himself. Double time, not bad."

"Funny how the time you were sick was just the time you wanted off, isn't it? Playing hooky Tommy?"

"Oh, so that's it," Tommy said, his voice suddenly hard and edged with anger. "You think I faked it. Is that what this is all about? What are you trying to say?"

"That's what I'm asking you Tommy. What's going on?"

"Look, I don't have to take this crap. The union agreement says anything over three days requires a doctor's certificate. Under that, a telephone call to the supervisor is required. I did that. I can't tell when my allergies are going to hit. What are you saying?" Tommy asked, rising in the chair, his voice hoarse with accusation.

"I'm just saying it's awfully coincidental."

91

"If you have any problem with me taking sick time when I'm sick, talk to the union steward," Johnson spat out. Then he turned and left the office, slamming the door on his way out.

A few minutes later, once he had cooled down, Gary called Human Resources asking to speak with someone familiar with Johnson's work record.

"You've got a real gem there," Marilyn Bolland said, as she studied data on Johnson's sick leave on the computer screen in front of her. "He has a pattern of sick leave that stands out from everyone else's. Usually two days at a time. There's one block of a week, but it's tagged with a doctor's slip. Tommy's quite a guy. He knows the union agreement inside out and he can quote chapter and verse from it. He plays it like a game."

"Can't you do something about it?"

"Not without a paper trail. There's no solid documentation in his file. You're the Supervisor, Gary. It starts with you."

Gary thought long and hard about the situation with Johnson. It bothered him to think that Johnson was using him and using the system to do what he wanted.

Later, when he was walking on the plant floor, he noticed Johnson talking with a small group of machine operators in the lunchroom. They were taking their coffee break. As he passed the windows that enclosed the lunchroom, he saw Johnson nod his head towards him as he spoke, and then the entire group broke into peals of laughter. Gary steeled himself and carried on with his observation of the work operation on the floor.

Thursday Dim Sum

"From what you've told me," Marty said, "this guy Johnson is one of your problem children. We all get them sooner or later. It comes with the territory. It seems to me though that he's familiar with the black art of dogging it."

"What do you mean?'

"He knows what he can get away with. I've met people like your Tommy Johnson. In their own peculiar way, they're oddly creative. They can quote chapter and verse from the

92

union agreement, but they're stretched when they have to do a bit of real work. That's why I call it a black art. Just think about it. It takes a lot of misplaced effort and twisted creativity to dodge work in a large organization like yours. He knows his limits and yours. He's one of those people who sees an organizational system as something to be used and abused. Who knows why? Maybe when he was a kid Santa brought his older brother bigger Christmas gifts. Some people are never satisfied with what they have, so they push at the limits."

"Sure sounds like Tommy Johnson," Gary said. "He's pushing at the limits and getting under my skin at the same time."

Marty glanced knowingly across the table at Raymond. "What you've got to remember is not to take it personally," Marty said. "If you take it personally, you react emotionally, and that's not good. Johnson may be abusing the system, but you can't prove it. You have to focus on areas that you can do something about. If he's not doing his job, that's what you can focus on."

"I'm not sure about that. I've been learning my own job over the last few weeks. I really haven't been looking at individual performance, not yet at least. But I will."

"Take it slowly," Marty said. "Some things aren't worth going after. You don't want to open up some black box that will swallow up all of your time and resources to prove someone was lying to you. It's not worth it. When you're ready, take a good, hard look at what your people are doing. If they're meeting their production targets, and keeping to work standards, then be content with that. If they're not, well then, that's a different issue. You can do something about that."

At the Plant

The phone rang. Gary listened as the Human Resources Manager asked to see him. "What's it about?"

"It concerns a complaint brought against Tommy Johnson. I'd prefer not to discuss it over the phone," she said.

"I'll be right there," Gary said.

93

Within twenty minutes Gary had been informed in detail about the Tommy Johnson complaint. He shook his head in a gesture of disgust and frustration. "So," he said, "the crux of the problem is this: Tommy Johnson is accused of sexually touching one of the new machine operator trainees, Tracey Wright, on two separate occasions while she was being trained. She's brought the complaint to Human Resources for action. You've presented it clearly. But what I'm not clear on are your expectations covering what my role is. I'll be frank. This is a first for me, and I don't know how to handle this. I want you to know I'll do whatever I can."

"Thanks Gary," Kate Playle, the Human Resources Manager said. "I really appreciate your help on this. Most of the Supervisors here don't want to touch these kinds of problems. They beg off, saying it's an HR thing. But the problem is closest to them. We can't really address it without close cooperation on the part of the Supervisors."

"So how do I start?"

"You meet with Tommy Johnson as soon as you can. You report on the facts that we've discussed here, and you ask for his version of the incident. Then you take notes on what was said. Based on that meeting, we can decide on the next steps. I think it's important for you to get his input before we escalate things. Are you O.K. with that?"

"I am."

"Good. I'd also like it if you reviewed this folder," Kate said, passing a blue plastic folder to him. "It contains information on our procedures for progressive discipline. You may find it useful to look at before your meeting with Johnson. Come and see me if you have any questions."

"Thanks, I will." Gary liked her matter-of-fact directness. Kate Playle was a wiry, strawberry blonde with a brusque businesslike manner that left you feeling everything had been attended to, and considered. Gary believed in confronting problems directly. He decided to review the Human Resources file and then meet with Tommy Johnson.

"Like I said, Tracey's accusation is a pile of crap. Look Gary, it's a simple thing. She was at the monitor, and I was behind her, giving instructions. I brushed against her, maybe, but that's it." Tommy Johnson's face was agitated and flushed.

"She said it happened twice, on separate occasions, and both times, she told you to stop it. She said you pressed yourself against her in a sexual way."

"Well, it's her word against mine. That's what it comes down to. Look, I don't want to talk about this anymore. It's a mistake that she made, that's all."

"Tommy, I want to give you a warning about sexually touching anyone on company premises. We have a zero-tolerance policy concerning that. Now, you say it was a mistake. That's fine. But, Tracey Wright says it happened twice. She has no reason to make it up. That's what bothers me."

"I don't care what bothers you. That doesn't matter to me at all. It didn't happen like she said, that's all. Now I'm leaving. If you want to talk about this again, I want my union rep here with me." Tommy Johnson abruptly stood up and left Gary's office.

Gary reached for his telephone. "Hi Jim, it's Gary. We've got a problem that I need to talk to you about."

"Can it wait?" Jim Ferris shot back, sounding annoyed.

"Nope, it can't." Gary spent the next few minutes informing his manager about the situation. When he had finished, he waited for Ferris to respond.

"I didn't need to hear this right now. I'm preparing my quarterly report for the board, and this is sure something I could do without. I don't need any of this."

"Neither did Tracey Wright," Gary said quietly. A long silence followed the comment, and then Gary could hear Ferris muttering something under his breath.

"You're right. I appreciate your informing me of the situation. I've got a voice message from Kate Playle, and I guess that's what it's all about. I'll give her a call right now. Thanks. I'll get back to you."

After the call Gary decided to do something he'd thought about for some time. Taking a small package from his desk, he left his office. He found Vinko Grubisic making some minor adjustments on his machine.

"Vinko, can I have a minute? It won't take long."

"Sure. What can I do?"

"You're doing it. You're doing a fine job in getting things rolling with our new floor configuration, and I just wanted to say thanks." Gary smiled and handed the package to Vinko who just stood there, surprised and motionless.

"Go ahead. Open it. It's for you."

Vinko carefully opened the gift. Gary watched as he unfolded the multi-purpose tool. He noticed that Vinko's eyes were suddenly moist with just the trace of tears.

"This is the first time, the very first time, I've ever received something for my work here. Thank you Gary."

"I just wanted to show my appreciation for what you've done." Suddenly, Gary felt a bit awkward at the show of emotion. "Keep it up," he said as he made his way down the line.

Over the next few weeks, Gary continued to fine-tune the production flow. He took pains to get at the small details of each machine operation asking questions to probe each and every facet of the individual machine operation and how it fit into the larger machine configuration on the floor. At the same time he was getting to know his staff as individuals, their likes and dislikes. Through his careful observations and countless questions, he was beginning to know the different motivations of his staff. Recognition was a big factor for many. A simple thank you was reward enough for some. For others the prospect of paid time off was a real incentive. He knew that Tommy Johnson was the exception, and he was grateful for that.

Kate Playle's urgent request to meet with her in her office had surprised Gary. She hadn't mentioned what it was all about. Somehow he knew that the issue was a Tommy

Johnson one. He chuckled to himself over his new-found psychic powers.

"Let me guess," Gary said, as he sat opposite Kate Playle in her cramped second floor office. "Could it be about my number one problem child, Tommy Johnson?"

Kate smiled grimly. "Unfortunately, yes. The situation has escalated. Let me give you an overview. Two other female staff from different departments have reported sexual harassment incidents. They decided to come forward after they heard through the grapevine that Tracey Wright had come to me with a complaint. My interviews with them have been detailed and thorough. I've had meetings with Jim Ferris and senior management, and also the union rep. I've drafted this letter to be signed by management. I wanted to keep you in the loop because Johnson reports directly to you. This letter here, as you know, is the second step in our progressive disciplinary procedure. The third step usually consists of more disciplinary interviews and follow-up letters, but I think that things are going to move very, very quickly now, given the latest complaints. We're almost at the fourth step, termination. Gary, I do believe, given the evidence, that Tommy Johnson will be terminated."

"It looks like Tommy's past is catching up with him."

"And none too soon," Kate said. "We've got a huge file on him, but he's crafty, and uses the union agreement like a game. But now, finally, we can put a stop to his shenanigans."

"And Ferris will sign the letter?"

"Yes. It's curious but I don't think he wanted to. The whole situation seemed to annoy him. At first, he said that it was strictly an HR thing, but I convinced him otherwise. His senior manager felt so too. SmarTech has a zero-tolerance policy on sexual harassment."

Later that day, Jim Ferris stomped into Gary's office as he was having lunch. Gary looked up from his tuna sandwich into Ferris's agitated face.

"So, you've become Santa Claus!" Ferris exclaimed. "I don't think I gave you the authority to use your department budget to buy gifts for employees."

"What are you talking about?" Gary said, putting his sandwich down with some reluctance.

"Vinko's little gift. We can't afford that kind of nonsense. He said it was the first gift he'd ever gotten from SmarTech. Besides, if you're going to do it for one, you have to do it for all. I don't want the union down my back."

"So that's what this is all about. Look Jim, I'm trying hard to meet those expectations we talked about. You told me you wanted a 30% increase in production. That's what I'm trying to do. And one thing you should know before you go any further. That small gift to Vinko came out of my own pocket. He's helping us to get that 30% increase. I wanted to show him my appreciation. I saw it as an incentive for him, a small token. I don't appreciate being accused of using our budget for something that I took it upon myself to do."

"I didn't know that," Ferris said, looking confused and stopped in his tracks. "You should have told me."

"You never have the time to talk about something like an incentive program. So, for me to get the increase we want, I have to treat my people right. That means recognizing their contributions and rewarding them when I can. They deserve that."

Ferris grimaced. "O.K., I hear you. Enough said. Has Kate Playle talked to you about Tommy Johnson?"

"Yeah."

"It looks like we've finally nailed him. I've checked with our legal people. He's out."

"I can't say I'm sorry to see him go."

"No one is," Ferris said. "I just wish it could have been done sooner. I think of discipline like surgery, like a surgeon's knife. You want the scalpel to be really sharp for cutting."

"I've never thought of it like that, but I suppose you're right. Hey, before you leave, can I show you something Vinko has suggested to cut some of our machine downtime?"

"You sure can. By the way, this picture, is that your daughter?"

"It is. That's Carly."

"A fine looking girl."

"Thanks Jim."

Thursday Dim Sum

"This dish is great. What's it called Raymond?"

"Those are phoenix paws, a great delicacy."

"I've never had anything like it before," Gary said.

"It melts in your mouth," Terry said as he poured another round of tea.

"What kind of meat is It?" Gary asked.

Raymond grinned. "Actually, they're chicken feet, chicken claws," he said, watching Gary's momentary look of surprise turn once again into delight.

"So Gary, from what you've told us, your work is going well. Tommy Johnson is gone, and you're closing in on that 30% production increase."

"Work is going great Raymond. Knock on wood. All of my staff are doing their best as far as I can see. Jim Ferris is even making noises about a formalized reward and recognition program. But I've got to tell you something. What I've discovered is that I can't get into someone's head to motivate them. What I can do though is create the kind of conditions or environment where they can choose to do their best and be motivated. I want to set goals and get people to strive for their best, like the top of Maslow's pyramid of needs. That's what it's all about. You have to keep your eyes and ears open and focus on individuals. Look for patterns. Keep on top of things."

Sylvie looked intrigued. "I'm curious about the kind of Supervisor or team leader that makes you? Are you a boss or are you a buddy?"

"It depends on the situation. I can be both. I have to be both. Let me tell you what I mean. With Tommy Johnson, the buddy approach would never work. He'd use it to his advantage. I had to be the boss with him. I didn't like it, but I had to maintain discipline and be in control. That's what's expected of me as a Supervisor, and that's what I'll do. It all depends on the situation."

Inukshuk Six: Motivate Staff & Maintain Discipline

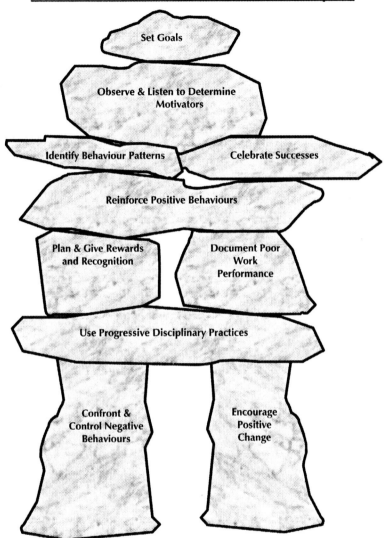

Set Goals

Observe & Listen to Determine Motivators

Identify Behaviour Patterns

Celebrate Successes

Reinforce Positive Behaviours

Plan & Give Rewards and Recognition

Document Poor Work Performance

Use Progressive Disciplinary Practices

Confront & Control Negative Behaviours

Encourage Positive Change

Super Skill: Manage Results through Effective Meetings

Profile Seven: Raymond Tang

Raymond receives input from the other supervisors on prioritizing his work and on managing results. He learns that the key to securing effective results is through meeting management. He sets about coaching his staff on this important supervisory competency.

Thursday Dim Sum

Raymond was watching closely as Terry carefully separated a few dim sum items on his plate. He observed Terry using a chopstick to mark off the areas for the shrimp dumpling, the beef ball, and the fried noodles respectively, and then methodically tasting each item in turn. He noticed that Terry ate his food in a clockwise manner. Raymond wondered if his approach to dining in this way was conscious or unconscious. What was obvious to him was that Terry enjoyed the food immensely. Raymond smiled in appreciation of his friend's meticulous dining style.

"So Raymond," Terry began, "it's your turn today. What is it you want to discuss?"

"Thanks for asking. I guess I'd like to find ways to focus on and manage results better. I get so caught up in situations and minor problems that crop up that I forget about the big picture, the results. Somehow, I need to do that better."

Terry glanced around the table. "Well then, I'll start things off. I think that the groundwork for focusing on results is all about managing time. If we're going to focus on results, we need to set priorities, and that involves making decisions about how we're going to spend our time. Our planning, our ability to organize around priorities, depends on how we use the time that we have available. Time is our basic resource. Raymond, I think you can begin by examining how your time is spent over a standard workweek. What I did involved keeping a time log for a few weeks. It has to be rigorous. I made sure the workweek was broken down into fifteen-minute chunks of time. I kept track of the smallest thing that threw my schedule off. If someone or something interrupted me, I noted down what it was. I had to be honest with myself. I didn't want to create a time log of how my workweek should be spent. I wanted to see how it actually was spent. There's a big difference."

Marty shrugged. "I know exactly what you mean about the fifteen minute chunks. I'm called upon to account for my time each and every week. My budget allocation depends on it."

"I like the time log idea," Raymond said, "but I've got to tell you, most of my time is spent reacting to problems in my department. Every time I've tried to plan my day, something just happens. A crisis, real or imagined, lands in my lap, or somebody doesn't show up for an important meeting. I'm under the gun all the time. More than half of my time is spent reacting to some crisis. I'm not complaining. I'm just telling you the way it is." Raymond looked around the table. Most of the others were nodding in agreement.

"That's just it," Terry said, "you need to know where your time is going... exactly where it's going. The time log will probably just confirm what you already know, but it's a start. It's just a diagnostic tool. But tell me, what do you do now as far as time management goes?"

"The usual things I guess. I prioritize what I think needs doing. You know, A, B, C priorities. The A's are the really important items, like deadlines. The B's are important but not essential. The C's are nice-to-do activities. I can break these categories down further by attaching numbers. You know, the standard practice. If there are a lot of A-priorities, I can label them A1, or A2, or A3. I do that, and it helps, but I'm still at the mercy of things over which I have no control, like inventory that just isn't there when I need it."

Terry leaned away from the table, allowing a waitress to clear the used dishes away. He waited until she was finished before he responded to Raymond.

"Setting priorities involves making decisions about how you're using your time. You're already doing that, and that's fundamental in getting the results you want. What I'm curious about Raymond is your remark about how so much of your time is spent in reacting to events. That's probably the most common argument I've heard. A lot of supervisors feel they just can't plan ahead given the amount of time they spend in reaction mode. There's an old saying: 'if you feel you can or can't, you're right.' That's where the change has to take place. We have to believe that planning our time around our priorities will make a difference."

"So you're telling me I don't have the right attitude. Is that what I'm hearing?" Raymond tried to sound offended but couldn't.

Terry chuckled. "I'm referring to supervisors in general. What I'm suggesting is that most supervisors don't give enough weight to their own priorities. I'm saying it's not enough to draw up lists of priorities. You have to commit to them and invest great importance to them. There's nothing wrong, I think, with a little healthy obsession. The things that are really important shouldn't be held hostage by the crises that erupt all the time."

"But you can't just ignore the problems and crises that come up. You have to deal with them, don't you think?"

"Sure you do. What I'm arguing for is flexibility with a little built in obsession. In order to focus on results, you have to be a little obsessive with the things that are really important. That doesn't mean ignoring the crises, but it does mean that you're like a bird dog for the really important long-term goals and plans that you have."

"It's really hard to do that Terry. I mean just think about it. I've got mounds of paperwork, endless meetings, and a steady stream of well-intentioned or not so well-intentioned visitors. It's not as easy as you're making it out to be. It's tough."

"I agree with everything you've said, especially concerning meetings. What I'd add to the mix is a little healthy obsession on the results you want."

"Are you serious about 'being obsessed,' as you put it?"

"Yes, but the obsession has to be flexible. I've found that unless a supervisor practices this obsessive quality, other things, other situations, take over control. Raymond, you've already told us how you're in reaction mode so often. The best way to counteract that is through being so focused on results that you're obsessed."

"Like Captain Ahab after Moby Dick," suggested Gary.

"No, not like that at all. Captain Ahab's obsession was desperate and fatal. Flexibility is the key to our discussion on obsession. I mean, you have your goals. They define the results you want. That's what should be driving you. Sure, you have to react to problems and situations that shoot up in front of you, and make the necessary changes to deal with them, but you can't be set off course by them. You have to keep focused. I think if you start focusing on meetings, on meeting management, just a bit obsessively, you'll be on the right track. "

"I don't follow you. What do you mean by meeting management? Are you talking about chairing a meeting?"

Terry paused for a moment, thinking about how to best communicate his subject.

Raymond was leaning forward in his chair, his thin frame angled towards Terry, waiting.

"I want to tell you that you can't think about meetings in the conventional sense. Most meetings just swallow up time the way a great white shark bumps into its prey and then devours it. Anything it bumps into is fair game. Think about it Raymond. How much time have you spent at meetings? What came of that investment in time?

"Just look at these gray hairs, the ones that are still hanging on," Raymond said, passing his hand over his balding gray hair.

"Better gray hairs than ulcers," Sylvie commented, her face animated and bright.

"Right on," Terry said, holding up two fingers to emphasize his next points. "Let's begin with two facts. The first: the average supervisor and technical professional spends one-fourth of their total work-week in meetings. Second fact: Over fifty per cent of the productivity of billions of meeting hours is wasted. Think about that. Now, what does that tell us about how we use the principal vehicle for making decisions in any business or organization? What does that tell us about managing results through meetings?"

"I've lived with that for a long time," Raymond said slowly. "It's just in the nature of meetings to be like that I guess. I try to do my best despite that. I'm sure we all do. I was hoping we could focus on something that's in my power to change, that's all."

"But that's my point," Terry said. "We can make meetings work if we have the right approach."

"How? Would you use surgery or a bomb?" Marty asked with a twinkle in his eye.

"Neither, once I know what needs to be discussed, I'd focus on four meeting goals, to help me get to the necessary decision if that's what needed to be done." Terry paused, taking a sip of his tea. "Boy, that's good tea," he said.

"O.K., I like the dramatic effect," Sylvie said, smiling broadly at Terry. "Now tell us what those goals are."

"Your wish, dear lady, is my command." Terry held up four fingers. "First of all, the goal of any meeting worth its salt is to coordinate and focus group or team effort. Second, to save time and reduce unnecessary conflicts. Third, to give clear expectations, and fourth and finally, to select the best structure to process information. That's it in a divine nutshell folks."

"You seem awfully sure of yourself," Sylvie said, her dimpled smile radiating goodwill.

"I learned the necessity of those four goals the hard way, through countless trials and errors, and heaps and heaps of frustration."

Gary laughed. "You know, I can sure relate to the clear expectations part. That's a sensible supervisory goal, and it seems to me just right that it's a meeting planner's goal as well."

"That's a good start," Raymond said. "The goals you mention are necessary especially for managing results. But not everything is within our control. There are problems that crop up again and again in meetings even when you have a strong chairman."

"Chairperson," Sylvie interjected.

"Yes, thank you Sylvie. Chairperson."

Terry nodded. "I agree that there are many problems with meetings, but control is the real issue behind ineffective meetings. That's what I want to discuss here. Meeting leaders have to be a bit obsessive on this point. Let's start by hearing what they are, the common problems that we all have."

"Most of the meetings I go to are too long," Marty began. "They usually start late because not everybody arrives on time. Then, there are interruptions, with people taking messages right there in the meeting, or leaving during the meeting. No wonder they always go overtime."

"Don't forget people jumping around different topics, and not even bothering with the agenda, if there is one," Sylvie said, using her hands expressively in the graceful way she had of reinforcing her points.

"And then there's the dysfunctional team," Raymond said. "That's what I've got right now, and I want to correct that before I retire. As individuals they're O.K., but get them together and watch out. They're paranoid about any little change to the status quo. It seems to me almost impossible to get and manage the results I need with a negative group like that. Mind you, it's only one of several departmental teams that report to me, but it's becoming a major problem. How can I change that?"

Terry twirled a chopstick with the fingers of his right hand. "I don't have all the answers, but I think I can help get things started."

"That's a problem in itself," Gary said. "Where do you start? A meeting has as many sides as a seal."

"Well, you can begin by determining the type of meeting. Are you going to pass along information on a decision that's already been made, or do want input before you make a decision? You see, the degree of decision sharing must be presented to the group from the very start. You have to give people expectations on what their role is. Are you asking them to give you input or recommendations that you or someone senior to you will make the decision on, or are you delegating decision making to the group? That can't be emphasized enough. People need to know what they're there for."

"What's the best way to do that?" Raymond asked.

"If you're the chairperson, you frame things, you give a short three to five minute orientation speech outlining the background, the meeting purpose, the degree of decision sharing, and any other need-to-know information. I think that those first few minutes are the most vital part of the whole meeting. If you do that right, you'll cut your meeting time in half, and set the stage for getting at the results or decision that you're after."

"Terry," Raymond said. " I have a request to make on a side issue. Would you mind preparing the inukshuk for this supervisory skill. I want to make sure all of the key elements are captured."

109

"Sure."

"Getting back to expectations," Gary said, "how do you do that?"

"Good question. Each participant at a meeting has to know what his role is. If they don't, or if they forget it, then it's the chairperson's job to set them straight. Every organization has their own style of conducting meetings. I think the best way of addressing expectations and a whole raft of other meeting-related issues from scheduling to decision making, is through a documented company policy on meetings. Now, don't get me wrong. I'm not a paper person. But I've found that a simple, accessible document on meetings can save an organization time and money. I'm talking tens of thousands of dollars, maybe more."

"Do you really think people would even bother reading it?" Gary asked.

"I make it a point to review our meeting policy with my staff regularly. I don't leave something as important as that to chance. It's really the source for an effective meeting. Just think about it. If you don't have some ground-rules that set guidelines for meetings, anything goes, and anything can happen. Let's face it, there's bound to be interruptions, and people will be coming and going as they please unless you have clear ground-rules. A policy on meetings forestalls many, many problem areas."

"It's just like my team meetings," Sylvie commented. "That's what I've started doing as team leader. I make sure we agree on how we communicate with each other, and what's acceptable, and what's not."

"Exactly," Terry said. "Most people think that how people meet, what I call meeting process, will look after itself. Most people just focus on meeting content, the agenda, but that's forgetting about process. You can't afford to do that. It's not rocket science, but it's got to be mastered."

"What about the agenda?" Marty asked.

"I don't think you can have an effective meeting without one. The best approach is to distribute an agenda in advance.

This way, people know what to expect and they can suggest changes, if need be, at the start of the meeting."

"Any special format?" Sylvie queried.

"Maybe. It depends on the organization and their preference. Some organizations have a template that they use, with columns for actions to be taken, and the people responsible, with deadlines, and other need-to-know information. There's a lot to be said for standardized agendas and meeting plans like that. I think it's a good idea. The thing is, you've got to go with whatever works in your organization, and keep on improving."

"Terry, you, Sylvie and Gary, are from blue-collar workplaces. Do you think this meeting approach will work as well in white-collar environments like Marty's and mine?"

"Of course. The goals and results may be different in the public sector, but you're still dealing with people and process just the same."

"I agree," Raymond said. "The results-based management model that we use in my workplace rests on the premise that we hold meetings that work, that get results."

"Is it a good model?" Does it work?" Sylvie asked.

"Yes, it works. Without getting into all kinds of definitions and jargon, it's a lot like a washing machine. You put clothes into the washer- call them inputs. These are your resources, what you start with. A transformation happens as a result of that activity. Then you're left with an output, clean clothes. One of the outcomes of that might be an improved appearance, and the overall impact, could result in all kinds of good things that can't be predicted immediately. I'm simplifying it of course, but essentially that's how I think of it. It's a system made up of many small processes that get you the results you want."

"Like clean clothes," Sylvie said.

"Just like that," Raymond said, with a smile.

"Time out," Terry cried out, using his hands to frame a T. "The dim sum cart' s coming around again. Raymond, help us out here. What do you think we should have?"

"Let's try the *cheun fun*, and the *cha siu pau*, for now," Raymond said, speaking to the waitress.

"C'mon Raymond. Give us an instant translation," Gary said, studying the contents of the dim sum baskets as the waitress removed the basket lids for the group to see what was inside.

"Sure thing. The *cheun fun* have shrimp or pork wrapped inside," Raymond said, pointing to the soft, white rolls, steamed and shiny. " We'll get two plates of each. I think you'll like them." The waitress set four plates on the table and sprinkled each with soya sauce. "Yes, and let's also have several of the *cha siu pau*, " Raymond said. "These are steamed buns stuffed with roast pork."

Terry swallowed in anticipation as the waitress placed the baskets down. The aroma was subtle and delightful. Raymond spoke rapidly in Cantonese to the waitress. "I've asked her to bring us a platter of steamed whole fish that we can share. It's not a dim sum item, but I think you'll be pleasantly surprised."

'I'll tell you something Raymond," Marty said. "There's no place I'd rather be right now than here."

"Me too," Sylvie added.

"Me three," Gary wisecracked.

"Oh that is bad," Terry said.

"Oh yes, it is," Gary replied, "but this is so good," as he ate a piece of the shiny white shrimp roll.

As they ate, the waitress refilled their teapots and cleared away the empty baskets. She also brought three tiny saucers filled with chili sauce. The chili sauce had become one of Terry's favorites. As he watched his friends enjoying the food, Raymond decided to propose a toast.

Raising his teacup, he began, "I wish to make this toast to good meals and good conversation."

The five of them raised their cups and then sipped and drank their tea in a thoughtful, contented silence. It was Sylvie who focused their attention on their elusive topic once again.

"My biggest problem is with team meetings. Frankly, most of them are dysfunctional with griping that doesn't stop, flashes of anger, and a total lack of anything you could call teamwork. It's not nearly as productive as it could be. Most of the meetings are a waste of time. Really, it's that bad. I sure could use a few suggestions."

"Well, " Terry answered, "you've given us a sense of what the symptoms are. So, start by asking them what's not working. Ask them for guidelines for better meetings."

"I don't want to give up all control," Sylvie said, her face suddenly sharp and strained at the thought of a free-for-all at the next meeting. "Besides, I don't want it to degenerate into a situation even worse than it has been."

"Start with the control issue," Terry said. "Your people have to know where they stand. What degree of decision sharing are you willing to allow? In the end, you have to report back to senior management. But, you owe it to your team to give them clear expectations on what will happen with their input, their recommendations. You may have to tell them that the degree of decision sharing will change according to what's on the table, but you have to make things clear. To do this, you need to focus on your decision-making processes, and later on, you need to follow up on meeting decisions and activities to see if they've been effective. That's the best way to evaluate the results you're focusing on."

"You know," Sylvie said, "I just might start calling you 'Doctor Meeting' from now on. I'll give it a try. After all, I've got nothing to lose but my frustration."

Raymond used the blunt end of his chopsticks to pick up one of the steamed pork buns from the dim sum basket. After placing it carefully on his plate, he said, "I just wish there was some way of harnessing all the energy used in resisting new ideas, in challenging things. Boy, would it make a difference in the quality of my meetings with staff. I mean that's better than people just going along with whatever I say, but conflict is too often unproductive."

"Then use the devil's advocate," Terry said.

"What do you mean?"

"Give someone the role of devil's advocate, someone who can adopt a positive role by criticizing the decision that you reach. This person challenges and tests all of the major assumptions and premises that inform your decision. It's an incredibly useful role for someone to play. Keep in mind that it's an assigned role by the group. It's not useful if someone arbitrarily decides to play the devil's advocate without sanctioning by the group. That can be counter-productive."

Raymond reflected on Terry's remarks. "It's worth a try. Even if it doesn't work, it sure can't be much worse than the situation I've got now."

"I don't think you'll be disappointed," Terry said, as the waitress placed the steaming fish on the table in front of them. It was sprinkled with green onions and looked delectable. Sylvie looked at Raymond and winked in appreciation.

At the Office

Raymond cleared his throat and began. "You have the agenda before you. The items are consistent with our goals for the quarter. Before we get into the discussion though, I want to give a brief five-minute orientation speech, an overview of my expectations based on the agenda. You'll notice that immediately after my presentation, I want to spend some time on defining our roles and responsibilities. Each of us has to know what the meeting expectations are for his or her role. So, let's get started."

After Raymond had finished his orientation speech, he asked each of the seven meeting participants to discuss what they believed their role entailed, round-robin fashion, and how they could advance the meeting's goals based on their role. He said that it was essential that the team work together on improving their meeting process.

Initially, a look of surprise came over everyone present. Eric Matalon smiled briefly and began: "Well, this is a first. I've never been asked to give what I think is my role in a meeting before. But since I'm starting things off, let's start with this," he said, raising the agenda high in the air and then putting it face-down in front of him. "The thing is, this agenda is great, but it would really help me prepare for the meeting if I had a copy in advance. I'd like to think about some of the issues beforehand, and maybe even suggest something to be included. Does that make any sense?"

"It sure does," Dave Clark said. " It will give us time to research things a bit. I'll second that. If we could have it a few days before, it would make a difference."

"But, getting back to roles and expectations," Eric said. "I think it's really important that if someone has an idea they want to share with the group, they have to take the time to organize it. A lot of the contributions are rambling and just not relevant."

Leaning forward against the table, Dave Clark hesitated and then began: "I think it's important that everyone has a chance to contribute ideas. I'd like to suggest to the Chairman that we somehow ensure that everyone has an equal amount of talk time. I don't know how we can do this exactly, but it's essential to get at the results we want. Raymond, you're the key person to make sure this happens. What do you think. Is it feasible?"

"I'll do my best to see that it does. One idea that I've heard about recently concerns the role of a devil's advocate, someone we can appoint to challenge decisions or assumptions that we base our decisions on. I'd like to suggest that we use this role at every decision-making meeting. It can work effectively as a rotating role, so that we all have a chance at it. This way, we'll make sure we've tested the decisions we come up with. Can I get agreement on this?"

"I'm with you on this."

'Me too."

"O.K. with me."

The rest of the team voiced their agreement. Raymond smiled. "I think we're on the right track. These suggestions will become part of our general meeting policy. Over the next few meetings, I'd also like to try out some facilitation tools, different activities we can use as a team to get at the information and ideas that we need to achieve the results we want. Is everyone O.K. with that?"

"Bring it on," Eric said, with a grin.

Inukshuk Seven: Manage Results through Effective Meetings

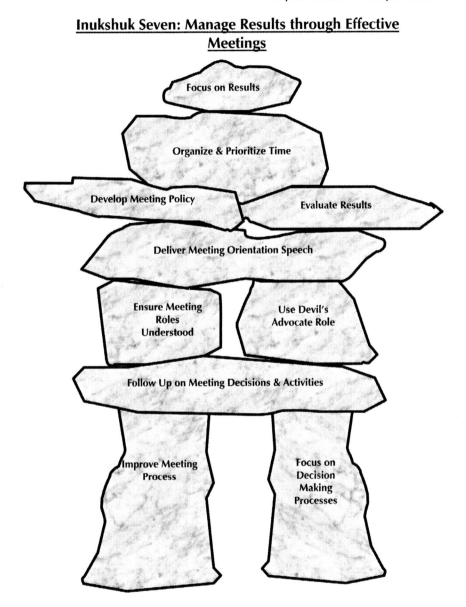

Super Skill: Coach and Develop Staff

Profile Eight: Terry Dunn

Terry sets about coaching some of his staff to assume some of his responsibilities. He discovers through discussions that coaching is a very effective way to manage employee performance and far superior to the traditional performance evaluation method. In addition to delegating some of his work, he ensures that some personnel receive specialized training in delivering on-the-job instruction. The coaching and employee development role is viewed as a fundamental supervisory skill, built on effective listening and questioning techniques, and one that essentially serves to influence behavior.

Thursday Dim Sum

"So," Terry began, "I've got my people trained. But, I want to keep an edge to them, to keep them learning and progressing. Anybody have any ideas on how I can help them?"

Marty leaned forward against the table with his palms face down against the white, plastic tablecloth. "At the stage you're at now, I'd suggest coaching. That's what we did as part of our change initiative, and boy, has it made a difference.

People are giving more at work, not because they have to, but because they want to."

"O.K.," Terry said, "let's start with a definition that helps explain what you mean. Coaching can mean different things to people."

"Sure. Coaching is something I understand as an ongoing process, a directive process, one that allows a supervisor to influence the behaviour of an employee through their efforts together. Boy, sounds impressive, doesn't it?"

"It's fine," Terry said. " I tuned into 'influence behaviour.' I take it that means I've got someone with an attitude problem, right?"

"It could be that, or it could be that there's a performance problem. Usually, it's an attitude or performance problem that requires coaching, or it could be someone who lacks enough knowledge about his or her job responsibilities. What it's all about is people development. Coaching is about giving feedback to people."

"That's what I'm interested in, " Terry said emphatically, "giving feedback, so that people know up front what I'm thinking about what they're doing. I've been in too many situations where the meaningful feedback only comes once a year at performance evaluation time."

"I feel the same way. Coaching is a tremendous way of sharing responsibilities, through delegating tasks, so that people feel trusted. It's a great motivator too."

Terry nodded. "I guess I don't know too much about it because I never got coached. You know, I don't know if that's good or bad. Maybe nobody thought I needed it."

Marty smiled. "Do you remember when Gary asked his manager for feedback on what was expected of him as a Supervisor? We talked a lot about the importance of clear expectations. What he could have used from the start was a good coach, a good supervisory coach."

"You got that right," Gary piped in.

Terry nodded in agreement. "So, what are the kinds of situations where coaching should be used?"

Marty leaned back in his chair and reflected for a moment. "Whew, when you think about it, you realize there are quite a few. Let's see. Job orientation would be one of the first, then on-the-job training. I know that when a new recruit comes into our detachment we have to explain some of the cultural things, you know, what to do, and what not to do. Sometimes, a person will need help in setting priorities to do their job better. Poor job performance is always a clear signal for a coaching strategy. In fact, I've always thought that coaching and performance management are one and the same thing. Then again, there are situations where someone needs coaching for a new position, or for a new work assignment. If self-confidence is an issue, coaching is certainly useful. I think that when you think about it, you realize that there are all sorts of situations that call for it. The main thing is to recognize when it would be useful, and then give the right kind of feedback. Do you know what I mean?"

"Yeah, I do," Terry said. "It's a one-on-one thing, supervisor to employee."

"Most of the time, I guess. But, you can have situations where an experienced employee is coaching another employee, or times when a supervisor is coaching several employees at the same time. I ran into that situation with our new file management system. I brought a group of supervisors together and coached them on how to handle the expected fallout from the new system. Getting and giving the right kind of feedback is the key to good coaching."

"I still don't know what you mean by feedback. Do you mean positive or negative comments?"

"Both, at different times in different situations." Marty gestured with his hands to emphasize his points. "You have to tell your people where they stand, what they're doing well, and what they need to improve. That's the rationale for feedback. Keep in mind though, that when you give feedback, there are three basic rules: make your feedback specific, make it well-timed, and make sure you've been understood. That's really the heart of performance management. What

I'm saying is that when you're giving feedback, whether it's good news or bad news, you have to make it specific. If you're giving negative information, describe the specific incident and suggest alternative behaviour. If it's positive, don't forget to comment on it. People deserve to hear that. Timing is everything. Feedback is best served warm, immediately after something happens or just before an employee is likely to repeat the behaviour. When all is said and done, when you've given your feedback, check to make sure that you've been understood."

"You make it sound easy, like common sense," Terry said, pouring tea into the empty cups in front of him. When he had finished serving and the teapot was empty, he removed the lid and placed it on the handle. He had learned the tactic from Raymond who had told him that it was a silent signal to the waitress to refill the teapot, a custom in many Chinese restaurants.

"It's just that, common sense, nothing more. Putting it into practice though is the hard part. It's also very uncommon. A lot of supervisors shy away from giving feedback. They're uncomfortable with it. It's important for supervisors to increase their comfort level."

"Something you said earlier really caught my attention. You said that coaching and performance management are the same thing. Can you speak to that a bit more?"

"Sure thing. I see the Supervisor as a coach, not a judge. That's why the Supervisor has to manage employee performance, not judge it like some two-bit dictator. Look, most of what passes for performance appraisal or evaluation is really based on little more than subjective feelings from a controlling, hierarchical point of view. That's why most people find the yearly performance review a pain in the neck, or worse. It's the most celebrated form of organizational torture devised by modern man. Just think about it. Most supervisors and managers shy away from it. The premise, the background thinking about it is all wrong-headed. Instead of judging someone, the time set aside for appraisals should be refocused as another opportunity for coaching, for performance management."

"That's refreshing to hear," Terry said, mentally thinking about the many, many times he had participated in the uncomfortable, and all too often, humiliating exercise of employee evaluation. He shook his head.

Marty laughed and looked around the table. "I guess all of you know about that."

Gary brushed back the hair from across his forehead. "But what about the performance appraisal, the evaluation. Are you saying to forget about it?"

Marty levelled his gaze at Gary. "I'm saying that the traditional approach to managing performance won't work. We've got to take a new tack on it. We've got to be coaches that help to release the potential of our people rather than bosses that control and restrict and judge. It's all about choice and selecting a better way."

"Wow," Gary said, "I never thought I'd hear that from a cop."

Marty leaned back in his chair and laughed. "It all comes back to how you view people at work. Don't get me wrong. There are a lot of police officers who still live by the old 'command and control' model of police work. I hold that people respond best to an open, collaborative approach. Quite apart from the specifics of the workplace, whether you work in a police detachment or in a car plant, it's how you view people at work, the model you hold, the fundamental thinking behind what you do, that's the important thing."

"But," Terry began, " it still comes down to evaluating your people at some point in time. You can't get away from that basic fact. You have to give feedback and assessment, and that can be a tough thing to do, when the feedback is negative."

'Terry, I want to put the emphasis where it belongs, on coaching, on performance management. Coaching is an ongoing process. It's real. It's something that goes on every day in an organization, or it should. Coaching is based on face-to-face relationships. Coaching is altogether different from evaluation. To my way of thinking, evaluation practices as they exist today, do real harm to an organization. The evaluation or appraisal interview usually only takes place once a year, if that, and hardly ever in upper management circles where it's too much of an embarrassment. Just think about it. How many people do you know look forward to it? I don't know of any. For most people it's a kind of bad joke that comes with the territory. Most people dread it, and rightly so."

"O.K., I'll grant you that," Terry said, "but management still expects me to do it, the evaluation thing. That's a clear and present expectation of being a supervisor. So, what do I do?"

"Fortunately," Marty replied, "you can coach. That's what you do. That's how you manage performance. You nurture it. You give feedback every day, and you get it back too. You focus on results in a collaborative way."

"Do you still use assessment forms in your performance management?"

"Yes, but the emphasis is on the collaborative relationship between the supervisor and the employee. It's the relationship that matters. That's at the heart of it all. The common focus is on the results wanted. My people need to know what's expected of them in terms of results, what they have to produce, and how those results will be measured. The supervisor has to manage employee performance to get at the results wanted. That's where the coaching comes in. If the employee can't achieve the results because of a lack of knowledge or skills or resources, the supervisor has to make sure that the missing parts are developed or supplied."

"So, you're saying it's a process of working together to get at the results wanted."

"Exactly. It's a continuous process, something that happens every day. It's not a one-shot thing. The supervisor and the employee are jointly responsible and accountable for achieving results, and for improving the process that determines how these results are achieved. Keep in mind that feedback is essential. Throughout the process, the supervisor has the responsibility of giving feedback and providing coaching. The employee has the responsibility for seeking feedback and for responding to identified issues. But remember, after all is said and done, after all the details, objectives, and responsibilities have been set and itemized, what really matters is the spirit behind the performance management process. It's the spirit of the relationship between the supervisor and the employee that's the really important thing."

Just then the waitress brought a fresh pot of tea to their table. Terry poured out a small cup of tea for everyone. There was a palpable feeling of contentment and satisfaction in the air. Marty took a sip of the steaming, fragrant jasmine tea and glanced around the table. Raymond was busy taking notes, quietly engrossed in structuring the discussion graphically. An inukshuk was beginning to take form.

"O.K., now for a few specifics, some tips that have helped me with the performance management process. You should have identified and agreed upon a number of objectives for the results you want, say between four and six. The number has to be manageable. These are the kind of things that are on the performance management form you asked about earlier Terry."

"That makes sense," Terry said. "Tangible results need to be identified. Otherwise, there aren't any clear expectations, and we've already talked about that."

"Sure, the other things to keep in mind are the performance indicators or measures. What I mean by that term are the ways in which the results for your objectives are going to be measured. It's important to agree on how results will be measured. None of these things, objectives, results, performance indicators, can be cast in concrete. Things change all the time. The important thing is to communicate continuously so that changes can be incorporated into your performance management strategy."

Gary brushed back a hank of his hair from his forehead. "Sorry guys, you're beginning to lose me. All of this sounds so abstract. Can you simplify it for me? Can you dumb it down?"

Marty nodded in agreement. "Sure thing. It's all about getting agreement on what your objectives and results are, and about how things are going to be measured. A checklist that I've found useful is the 'SMART' checklist. It's a concept that's been around awhile. Each of the letters stands for a key question to ask of your objectives and measures, your performance indicators. In other words, are your objectives and measures: specific?; measurable?; attainable?; realistic?; time-based?"

"I like that," Gary said. "It's something I can use. I like that very much. Smart."

Terry chuckled. "It's a smart process, with the emphasis being on the word 'process.' Marty's take on coaching, on performance management, is an ongoing process between the supervisor and the employee. That process is all about communication. That's based on a real, everyday, face-to-face relationship. Without that, and the common respect between both, nothing much is going to happen."

Marty raised his cup towards Terry, in salute. "I couldn't agree with you more. That's what it's all about, something you can't put on an appraisal form. It's the spirit of the relationship that counts."

Terry looked closely at Gary. "You know, my dad wasn't a very talkative man, but something he said to me has stayed with me all these years. The advice he gave me was this: 'practice public relations.' What he meant was that the most important factor in success was good public relations, good relationships between people. That's what effective supervision is all about: good relationships."

"Yup," Marty said, "that's the heart of it... good relationships. But now I want to talk more about the process, about how you can make monitoring performance more effective. It's not a one-time thing. Too many supervisors and managers just think of performance management as an annual exercise, a painful necessity that has to be done no matter what. But the thing is, it doesn't have to be like that. It's meant to be an ongoing process, a coaching process, one that focuses on improving performance. It seems to me that if a supervisor conducts short, regular debriefs with an employee throughout the year, that's the ticket."

"What exactly do you do in these debriefing sessions?" Terry asked.

"A number of things. Mainly, it's keeping track of performance in relation to the objectives and expected results. It's about feedback to let people know what they're doing right, and what to change if there's a problem or a block of some kind. The employee may need additional resources that the Supervisor isn't aware of. There are all kinds of things that can interfere with good performance, all kinds of variables. That's the reason behind these regular monitoring check-ins, these debriefs. If there aren't any discussions or communication about what's working and what isn't, something's going to get bunged up."

"But isn't that like micro-managing?" Gary asked. " I mean the employee knows the objectives and results that are wanted. He knows how these results are going to be measured by the Supervisor. So why so many additional meetings? I mean the employee isn't like my six-year-old who has to be continually watched. Nobody likes overkill."

Marty nodded. "I hear what you're saying, but I believe that if your objectives, your results, are important to you, you'll want to take the time, the necessary time, to check on progress. Keep in mind these check-ins aren't formal meetings. They can be five or ten minutes only, and you can use a one-page checklist to cover what needs to be covered. The monitoring is something you can do standing up on a plant floor. The important thing is consistency. The Supervisor is there as a coach. It shouldn't be a 'sink or swim' scenario. You want to help the employee as much as possible."

"O.K., I like the idea of these debriefing sessions, and the checklist. But it seems to me that it could be threatening to some people."

"It shouldn't be threatening at all if the Supervisor has taken the time to put the employee at ease by being warm and friendly. To my way of thinking, that's essential. Even in the busiest work environment, if you forget to be human in your interaction with others, you've lost it. But, it's not something you can just put on for a few minutes. You've got to be sincerely inviting, or people will put up their defenses." Marty paused for a few seconds to emphasize his point. He smiled and looked directly at Terry, waiting for Terry to continue.

"So, you've got your checklist, your SMART objectives, and you review them with the employee. How do you handle problem areas?"

"You start by describing the performance problem or area that needs improvement, and you define its impact on you, the employee, the department, and the company. Once you've addressed that, you listen to the employee. You hear them out. You listen for facts. You listen to their feelings about it as well. You've got to let the employee know you're interested in their opinion on ways to improve performance. You can do this by asking open-ended questions that help to draw out their suggestions. That's what you've got to build on, the employee's ideas on how to solve the problem. That's the bridge. You can offer suggestions when it's appropriate, but you want them to take responsibility. Based on that, you can agree on the actions for him or her to take, and then schedule a follow-up meeting to provide more feedback on progress. Keep in mind, it's coaching for results."

Terry nodded. "I like it. I'll use it. What's the word they use in HR? It's 'empowering.'"

Marty nodded. "It's empowering because it's human. It's about the Supervisor as a coach, and not a 'boss' in the bad sense of that word."

At the Plant

Terry approached Abdul Ali, the best machine operator on the plant floor, to ask him how his on-the-job training was going. Abdul was a tall, intense man with a shock of white hair that gave him more the look of an English professor than a machine specialist. The people Abdul was overseeing had finished the off-the-job training supplied by the equipment vendors, but there was much more to be done to ensure full competency on the job. Abdul always referred to his on-the-job training as coaching. Terry wanted to know precisely how he was conducting the training.

"What I do is fairly simple, but I have to make sure everyone understands the process involved," Abdul began. "We use five steps in all. The first step is preparation. My job is to make sure everyone is comfortable with learning on the job. I try to make them feel at ease. That's very important. I walk them through the overall operation, how the machine they're responsible for connects with the others on the line. I find out what they already know. I don't take anything for granted. I show them what's expected of all the machines on the line, and the one they're looking after in particular. I show them the output of their machine and how it contributes to the final product, what comes out at the end of the line. Then, as part of the preparation stage, I position them on my right, so that they have a clear, unobstructed view of the machine in front of them. Before we begin, I ask them to hold any questions they have until later, after the demo."

"Abdul, I've got a couple of questions. Do you have any particular reason why you want the person to your right? And why do you hold any questions until the end?"

"Well, as for trainee placement, think of it this way. When you were learning how to tie a necktie, it's easier for you to catch on if we're side by side, and not opposite each other. It's a lot easier. And, as for questions, it's better to hold them until after the demonstration. But, if they have a question or two, after the preparation phase, about the overall operation or product, it's good to deal with those."

129

"O.K., what happens next?"

"Step Two is the trainer demonstration phase. The trainer or coach demonstrates and explains the job or machine operation in a step-by-step fashion. I do this three times. Here's the breakdown of step two. First, I show and tell them 'what' it's all about. The learner observes and listens. Second, I show and tell them 'what and how.' Again, the learner just watches and listens. Finally, I show and tell them the 'what, how, and why' of the operation. Throughout the three repetitions, the learner just observes and listens. It's repetitive, but it works."

"I notice that you've got a job breakdown sheet posted here on the side of the machine. Is that the actual sequence you follow in your demonstration?"

"Yes, it's a memory aid. If I'm not right on the spot, the trainee can look at this simple graphic aid. It's color coded to match each step of the job operation. People like it."

"O.K., what happens next? Does the trainee go through everything you've demonstrated to see if it was learned?"

"Not quite yet. Step Three is the partial tryout. Here's how it works. The learner tells me what to do, and then I, as the trainer, show him what to do, based on what he's told me. The next step has the learner telling me the 'what' and 'how' of the operation without him actually doing anything. Based on what he's said, I show 'what' and 'how.' The final step of stage three involves the learner telling me 'what, how, and why'. After he's done that, I show him 'what, how, and why.' This way, I've got the learner in the position of taking the initiative by telling me what to do before I demonstrate based on the information he's given me. He's got to recall the right steps. If he doesn't, I use questions to get back on track. It's a step-by-step approach. Using questions is really important. It's systematic. Any mistakes or errors are all part of the learning during this stage."

"I think I get it. The 'what' refers to the steps involved in the job operation. The 'how' refers to the skills in doing it. The 'why' specifies the reasons behind it all."

"That's it Terry. It's the same stepped sequence that's followed in Step Four, the complete learner tryout step. That's where the learner begins by telling and showing the 'what' while the trainer listens, observes and questions when necessary. Then, the learner tells and shows the 'what' and 'how' with the trainer following up again with any necessary questions. This step is concluded with the learner telling and showing 'what,' 'how,' and 'why.' The trainer, as before, just listens, observes, and questions between the telling and showing parts of the learner's complete tryout. Follow me?"

"Sure do. It's simple enough, as long as you remember the different steps, and don't mind a bit of repetition."

"The repetition is important. You want it to be like a habit. Repetition is fundamental to effective learning."

"I like the approach Abdul. It's systematic and comprehensive. One question: do you follow up to check on how people are doing after a while?"

"That's the last step, Step Five. That's where the follow-up happens. I encourage each trainee to ask questions, lots and lots of questions. I also keep a log of all my trainees. It indicates, depending on the shift, the person they should go to for help when they need it. I check on their performance quite a bit at first, and then that tapers off as they become more and more proficient. There's an old saying that goes, 'you don't really know a thing until you've practiced every part of it thoroughly.' That's what this last step is all about: practice."

Terry nodded, impressed with Abdul's approach. "Any drawbacks to this five-step approach?" Terry asked.

Abdul shook his head. "None that I can see. You have to remember it takes time up front, the necessary time, for people to learn on-the-job. My job, as I see it, is to create the conditions for the learner to learn as much as he can in the time we have together. That's my job as a coach and trainer. The five-step method is like shingling a roof. You go over each part of the roof again and again, overlapping one with the other until you have a seamless, weatherproof roof. "

"I can see what you mean by the emphasis on practice, supervised practice, or coaching as you call it. It makes sense."

"It also works. It's the best way I know of to make sure the learning sticks. I want each of the different shifts to know and practice the same proven sequence of how to run a machine. I want them to feel comfortable with the whole operation. That's why it's so important they know the reasons behind the steps we follow. If a person understands why they're doing a certain operation in a precise sequence, they'll be better at what they're doing."

"Thanks for the lesson, Abdul. Say, would you mind coaching a few other trainers in your on-the-job training methods. I have a few people in mind as trainers. It will give us a consistency we haven't had in the past if I delegate that responsibility to them. That way, we'll make sure the learning sticks from the classroom to the plant floor."

"Anytime. Just let me know when you're ready."

Terry nodded in thanks and walked back to his office with a keener appreciation of coaching as a multi-faceted and sharply invigorating way to positively influence and develop employees. Like so many other things, he thought, the spirit of the relationship was the important thing. That was something that the best checklists couldn't ever hope to aspire to- the spirit of a working relationship that was built on trust and respect. He made a mental note to call Raymond and share some of his learning so that Raymond could include them in his graphic notes, the inukshuks.

A few weeks later Terry made a presentation to the management team on the coaching that was taking place on the plant floor. He spoke about coaching in two fundamentally related ways: coaching as a means of giving practical job instruction on a piece of machinery or work process, and coaching as a performance management process. For the first time in a long while Terry felt confident about the direction his supervision was taking. Systems were in place, and they were working. Driving home from work one evening Terry noticed the first star in the night sky. Soon, other stars were visible. All of them connected, he thought, even the ones he couldn't see. He smiled and thought about the systems that were in place in his own work environment. He felt connected. He started humming a joyful tune he hadn't thought about in a decade. The song carried him all the way home.

Inukshuk Eight : Coach and Develop Staff

Define Coaching

Manage Employee Performance

Give and Receive Feedback

Conduct Debriefs

Identify Key Objectives and Results Wanted

Apply SMART Checklist

Define Key Performance Indicators

Apply 5-Step On-the-Job Coaching Method

Listen for Fact and Feelings

Use Questions Effectively

Super Skill: Communicate: Listen, then Present

Profile Nine: Marty Hessler

Marty builds on his listening skills through learning approaches and techniques that focus on gathering information clearly and concisely. Sylvie explains the importance of background thinking and profiling an audience when making a presentation. Ways of organizing a presentation are discussed. The importance of communicating with skill in everyday situations is examined.

Thursday Dim Sum

Marty looked around the table appreciatively. All of the dishes had been cleared away, and they were enjoying tea. He was musing over the fact that he was learning more about supervisory skills in a Chinese restaurant than he had ever learned anywhere else. Marty loved the irony in that fact. He decided to bring up an issue that he was thinking about more and more.

Leaning forward against the table with his elbows, the way he always did when he had something to say, he began. "I don't know about any of you, but I sure wish I could listen better, you know, more effectively. In police work, it's a critical skill, especially during investigations. I just don't seem to retain everything."

"Like a lot of things," Gary said, "it improves with practice, conscious practice. I really believe that you don't know a thing until you've practiced every part of it thoroughly. When I was in sales, I really had to focus on what my clients were saying, on what their needs were. I found out that when I didn't listen, I lost business. And even when I understood the need to listen better, I still had to get over all of the things that interfered and blocked my listening, my attentiveness. "

Marty noticed that as Gary was speaking, he leaned his body towards him and looked directly into his eyes, making Marty feel he was really keen on discussing the topic. "The thing about listening," Gary said, "is that you take it for granted. Just because a person has normal hearing ability doesn't mean they listen well. I learned that from my six-year old daughter Carly. She kept telling me, 'dad, you're not listening to me,' and she was right. She'd be right there, sitting next to me in the car, talking away, and I'd be hearing her on some level, but not really listening. My mind was on a thousand different things from thinking about work to what I was going to cook for her that night. Listening, I found out, takes work, hard work."

"I know what you mean," Marty said. "I listen a lot better at work than I do at home. At least that's what my wife tells me. Things get in the way I guess. I mean I have a tendency to get distracted easily."

"Most people do. One fact that I came across at a sales seminar that I never forgot was that we can listen, on the average, at about three times the speed that we can speak. That difference leaves us time to think about what we're going to say next. It also means that we can block out what the other person is saying. Good listeners are rare. Just think about it. Not once in public school or high school or even college was I ever offered a course in listening. It's just assumed that everyone's got it. "

Marty leaned forward. "So what's your approach? How do you listen?"

"I go into what I call listening mode," Gary said. "I literally relax and block out any distractions, like a loud tie or a nervous tic. It's so easy to focus on some small surface detail, on appearance, rather than ideas. I give the person time to develop what they have to say by not interrupting, and then I check to see if what I heard was what the speaker intended to say. If I'm not sure about something that was said, I ask for clarification."

"How do you do that?"

"By paraphrasing or summarizing. I repeat back to the speaker what I thought was said, in my own words, and then I ask for confirmation."

"No special techniques?"

"Well like I said, my listening mode, my attitude, is what counts the most. Listening has to be a conscious effort. People pick up on that. They know when you're really listening. In the end, it's important to remember that the questions you ask about what you heard are critical. That's what makes my listening mode proactive: I ask questions. I've noticed that a lot of people don't do that. They may hear, but they don't really understand."

"What kinds of questions are you thinking of?" Terry asked. He noticed that Raymond was drawing one of his inukshuks.

"I like to think of questions as probes. I use them to get at additional information, to see what evidence there is behind the speaker's argument or presentation. Most speakers want you to do something with the information they're giving you. Formulating questions in my mind, as I'm listening, gives me an edge."

"Don't you find though that your attention wanders. I mean some people just go on and on. It's really hard to listen efficiently when the speaker doesn't know when to quit."

"Look, listening is hard work," Gary said. " It's natural for your concentration and attention to move in and out as your interest intensifies or wanes. That's just the way it is.

Most people listen at about a twenty-five per cent efficiency rate. I got that fact from a workshop I attended. Think about it. Twenty five per cent isn't very good. Effective listening is about effective communication. I really believe that effective communication, like electricity, has to have a closed circuit to work. If communication is common understanding, then it stands to reason that when we join the speaker in seeking understanding, we help to close the circuit."

"That makes sense," Marty said. He took a long, slow sip of his tea. He could smell the jasmine. "What do you think it is though, that gets in the way of people communicating? Can we get past the blocks?"

"I know we can. I did. After all, the blocks, or barriers, are easy enough to understand. Most people tune out from listening effectively because they think they know what the speaker is going to say. Instead of using the extra time they have to really probe what the speaker is saying, they plan what they're going to say next, especially if they have ideas that conflict with the speaker's. Then too, a listener can be distracted by their own preoccupations, you know, what they're going to do after work, or on the weekend. Mentally thinking about a golf game you're going to play can sure interfere with what someone standing in front of you has to say."

"Well, I'll give it a try Gary. I'll adopt the listening attitude you've been talking about, and then use questions as probes to focus on what's being said."

"A good listener is as rare as a phoenix," Gary quipped.

"What's that?" Marty queried.

"See what I mean."

"Here's the situation. More and more in my job I'm being called on to make presentations, even impromptu presentations at meetings. But I've got to tell you, it scares the heck out of me. The minute I'm called on to speak, my palms get sweaty, my stomach churns, and my mind goes blank. You'd think I was going to my own execution. Go figure. Being able to present information persuasively is a big part of what my job is all about, and sometimes I almost blow it.

The thing is, I know my stuff. I know the content by heart, but my delivery sure leaves a lot to be desired." Marty looked so vulnerable when he made his remarks that Sylvie touched his forearm lightly in sympathy.

"You know," Sylvie said, "it gets a lot easier with practice. I've read that making a presentation is one of the greatest fears that most people have. I know I did too, at first. But I got over it. I had to. The fear was interfering with my job, and I couldn't afford that."

"So what did you do? How did you get over it?" Marty asked.

"Not any one thing in particular. But by doing a lot of little things, only doing them more often. I'd give myself a treat if I volunteered for a presentation, or if I spoke up at a meeting. A new scarf, or a pair of jeans. If you really want to know the secret, it's attitude that does it. Oh sure, you have to be well organized and deliver well, but it's your core thought that makes all the difference."

"What do you mean by core thought?" Marty queried.

"Attitude. I tell myself that what I want to get across to my audience is very, very important. It's like giving someone a gift. That's the idea I hold in the back of my mind, the foundation thought, the core thought. That's the source of it all. Oh sure, I have to be well prepared and have my presentation structured for people to understand and remember it, but like I said, the main thing is attitude. If I'm as positive as I can be, and if I believe that what I'm presenting will be of great benefit to my audience, then I know I don't have to worry about being afraid."

"You mean it's sort of like a mind game," Marty said. "Getting the right attitude, preparing yourself, it's an inner game."

"Sure, you can choose to see it like that. But you have to believe it. If you fake it, you'll be found out. The important thing is a positive mindset. Everything else builds on that." Sylvie took a long, slow sip of jasmine tea.

"What's next?" Marty asked.

"Your purpose. What is it you want to do? Do you want to give some information out, or persuade, or whatever? People want to know things that are relevant to them and their situation. Remember too much information, especially irrelevant information, bloats a person's ability to listen. You have to define your purpose, and do it in one sentence. Otherwise, you'll be rambling. I always write out a purpose statement and proceed from there. Keep in mind that your purpose has to be conditioned by the group or audience you'll be addressing. I always profile the group I'm going to be speaking to. By profiling, I mean getting a sense of the general make-up of the audience. Who are they? What do they have in common? What's their background like? What benefits will they be able to take from what I have to say? Doing this makes a big difference to my comfort level. I view profiling as a kind of insurance. It keeps me on track and focused."

"That makes sense to me. You have to know who you're talking to, and how much information you can cover in the time you've got. I mean, by the time I've done the research on my presentation, I've got a real stack of notes in front of me. I have to really leave out a lot of information. I usually hand-write it out first and then make a typed version, word for word, of what I'm going to say. That way I can practice and see how close I am to keeping to my time limits. The trouble is, I always go over my time allocation when I'm actually presenting, especially if there are questions. Time seems to pass more quickly when I'm giving a presentation than when I'm just practicing the same presentation. Do you know what I mean Sylvie?"

"Yes I do, and I want to talk about that. The sharp anxiety that you may feel before and during a presentation can really alter a person's sense of time. When you're under the spotlight, it's hard to focus on your script. You can easily get sidetracked if someone asks a question. You can lose sense of where you were."

"But if I don't write it out word for word, what do I do? I can't memorize the whole thing. It's not poetry," Marty said.

"I'd suggest you use key words to trigger your memory. I'm not talking about a word for word memorization. I think the best way to go about it is to jot down key words that signal and mark your key points. All you really need are a few note cards. It took me a long time to realize that an effective presentation is built around three to seven points. It seems to me that seven points are the top limit. It's a lot like remembering telephone numbers. After seven, forget it. Think about it. If you want people to listen to you effectively and remember what you've said, you've got to help them by keeping it simple. A few points, well presented, are all you need. Your points should be like memory pegs, ideas that stick in someone's mind. If you have facts you want to present, make them jump out at your audience. Tell a story. The best presentations are based on telling a story. At least that's what I remember best. How about you?"

"Yeah, I like stories, but to tell you the truth, I don't feel confident enough to do that. I'm more concerned with organizing my presentation. Tell me more about that. Say I've selected my points, three to seven like you suggest. What else can I do to organize what I have to say?"

"There are a lot of different ways. One of the simplest is chronological: past, present, and future. It's as simple as that. Or sequential: first, second, and third. Then again, if you're looking at several options, you can outline them, and then give your recommendation. The important thing is to choose a pattern that best fits with your material. A good PowerPoint presentation lends itself to a structured approach like this."

"I'm going to be presenting on change. Basically, I'm talking about old ways and new ways of managing information. I guess the chronological system would be the best, right?"

"Maybe, but you could also compare and contrast those different approaches, or you could look at the positive aspects of the change as opposed to the negatives. What I'm saying is that you can use different ways of organizing what you have to say about change. You're not restricted to one way."

"You're telling me that I have a lot of options."

"You sure do. You know, one of my instructors told me about a 'memory palace' method. It seems that a fellow named Matteo Ricci suggested that people could remember lengthy presentations by imagining a mental structure, like a building, big or small, and then, while they're giving their actual presentation, they're also taking a mental walk through this imaginary building. In different rooms, they'd place an image of something they wanted to remember, an assigned position. Then they'd recall each of the ideas as they walked through the rooms and corridors of this imaginary building in their head. I've tried it. It works."

"That's cool," Gary said.

"O.K., I'm more comfortable about organizing my material now, but I'm still worried about being nervous. A lot of times I've known what I had to say inside-out, but I was still jittery. I kept on losing my train of thought. I just couldn't relax." Marty turned to Raymond and asked, "What about you, what did you do to get over your fear of speaking in public?'

"I just got older I guess. I got to the point where it didn't make sense for me to be nervous anymore. I was too old for that nonsense" Raymond chuckled. "That's not very helpful, but it's true."

"It's a mind game," Sylvie said. "You have to experience the fear, and then let it go. I know a speaker who uses visualization. That's a technique used to imagine yourself giving a good presentation. He sees himself delivering his presentation in detail, including the room he'll be in, and the clothes he'll be wearing. Another person I know swears by a lucky sweater she wears. Besides, a little nervousness is necessary, and I think, useful. You can see it as a form of energy that has to be converted to good uses. I always remember the line someone gave me: 'It's all right to feel butterflies in your stomach- as long as they're flying in formation.'"

Marty leaned forward resting his forearms on the table. "Everything you've said is good. I know it's true. But even at the best of times I lose my train of thought and get all flustered."

Sylvie noticed that as Marty spoke about his nervousness his face grew very strained and pale. She smiled. "One of the surest ways of keeping on track and confident is to listen to yourself."

"What do you mean?"

"If you take the time and the trouble to listen to yourself, to what you're saying, and to how you're saying it, things change for you. A lot of speakers don't listen to themselves. They just go on and on. They might as well be mumbling underwater. Try it, and you'll see what I mean."

Raymond signaled with his hand. "Sylvie, something you said earlier I'm not sure about. The core thought. What do you mean by it? How can you keep a certain attitude in your mind? It's one thing to have a good attitude when you're standing in front of a mirror practicing what you're going to say. It's another thing to try to keep that attitude in mind when you've got a roomful of people hanging on your every word."

"Right on. I use the core thought to keep me relaxed and confident. It's like a mantra. 'Be relaxed under pressure,' or 'think positive.' Something like that. I even write it down. It's what I think about just before I have to speak. Your core thought infuses everything else. I think of it as a protective coating for myself, like teflon on a frying pan. Try it out. See if it works for you."

The Presentation

Marty's time had come. It was his first coaching presentation with the supervisors in the neighbouring detachment. He felt sick just waiting for the workshop to begin. The consultant he was giving the session with, Jim Randall, looked cool and confident. He remembered what Sylvie had said, and he had practiced it thoroughly. His core thought was simple: focus on the positive. He intended to do that. His PowerPoint presentation reinforced the outline he planned to follow. He also had a few examples and personal anecdotes that the supervisors would be able to relate to. In his preparations he had profiled the supervisors, and he knew what would be important for them to know. He had concentrated on the benefits of the new information management system, the practical advantages to using it over the old, outdated manual system. The benefits listed on the overheads seemed to issue directly from his core thought: focus on the positive.

Marty glanced at his notes. He had rehearsed his presentation using one of Sylvie's suggestions. He would cover his key points by mentally walking through a building he had imaginatively constructed. Each of the rooms contained an image that called up the key point he wished to deliver. The first room contained a small table and on the table was a wrapped gift, the image he had created for eliciting the expectations of the group seated before him.

"We'd like to start with your expectations of the session."

Once he had begun, Marty took care to move slowly through his presentation, moving from room to room in his mind, recalling his key ideas from the images he had positioned in the rooms. He listened carefully to himself as he spoke, observing his audience and their reactions to his presentation. Behind everything he said, there was the background thought he had chosen: focus on the positive. That was exactly what he did. He felt a growing confidence, a belief in himself and in what he was doing.

In his mind's eye he entered a room with the image of a pear tree in the center. Each of the golden pears hanging from the tree represented a benefit of the new information management system. He began discussing these benefits in turn, imaginatively moving from branch to branch. At the same time he opened his PowerPoint presentation and the information on the slides mirrored the ideas he was discussing.

From the rapt expressions on the faces of the participants, Marty could see that the presentation process was working. He kept to his agenda, literally and imaginatively walking through it, but he also experienced the frustration that some of the supervisors felt about yet another brainstorm from Headquarters. Every now and then they vented that frustration on him. When Jim Randall had talked about change and the resistance issue, it was merely a concept. But here, resistance was in his face and visceral in the sometimes bitter comments of the supervisory group. Oddly, he thought, he was comfortable with it. He moved with it, anticipating it, and countered it with a recitation of the benefits of the change. Marty believed in the change and continued to focus on the positive. He gave a strong, committed presentation.

Thursday Dim Sum

"I can see why you're a police officer," Sylvie began. "You've given us a very detailed account of your presentation with the consultant. It went well."

"It did. I remembered to listen, especially to myself as I was presenting. I just wish I could do that all the time- communicate I mean. It's hard work, but you get results."

"I like to think of it as a lubricant, like oil to a fine machine," Raymond said. "Communication is the best way I know of to maintain professional working relationships."

Terry nodded in agreement as he savoured some delectable steamed ginger squid. Raymond noted with satisfaction that Terry was getting quite adept with chopsticks. He had used the blunt, thicker end of the chopsticks to select a portion from the dim sum basket containing the squid. He was learning the niceties of dim sum etiquette.

"Personal ones too," Sylvie added.

"Yeah," Gary said. "The key operative word is maintenance. Too often people forget that communication is essential to the maintenance of a host of interpersonal relationships. Without it, you can't really accomplish anything with a working group."

"Right on," Marty said. "The thing I've learned is that communicating through listening and speaking really needs our attention. Lately I've been focusing on formal speaking skills, on presenting, and also on formal listening skills, on attending closely to what someone is saying. But, we're communicating informally all the time. That's the thing. We need to bring the skills we use in formal situations into play. Just like we're doing here at our dim sum meetings."

Raymond looked up sharply from the inukshuk he was drawing. "That's it," he said. "In everyday situations, whether at work or not, we have to communicate skillfully."

"That sounds like a hard slog," Terry said. "I mean, it sure would be hard to keep it up all the time. I don't think it's doable."

"But it would get easier by doing it all the time," Raymond countered. "Like anything. You keep on doing it until it becomes a natural part of you, like breathing."

"Give me an example of what you mean," Terry said.

"Well, you start in little ways. If you're listening to someone, anyone, you make it a point to distinguish between fact and feeling. You sort out the facts, things that can be verified, from the feelings about those facts. Feelings have to do with drawing inferences and judgements. Do you see what I mean?"

"Yeah, I do. But it's going to be hard work to do that." Terry said.

Marty leaned forward against the table. "It's about being proactive and not reactive. You have to try things, take risks. I don't know if this makes any sense to you, but what I do when I want to change something in myself is this. I pretend to be someone smarter than myself. What I mean is, I imagine a person like myself, only smarter, and I ask what would he do in this situation? Then I do it."

"I agree," Gary said. "And your approach is an innovative one. Communication skills shouldn't be something you reserve for meetings or formal presentations only. It has to be fundamental to any interaction. We're always presenting when we speak. It may not always be a formal presentation, but it's a presentation nevertheless. You have to practice it like any other skill. I like it. That's what I do."

"How do you do that?" Terry asked.

"I did it by listening to Carly, my six-year old. You may laugh, but that's how I got started. Try listening, really listening to a child. It takes careful attention. The thing is, Carly is more important to me than anything else in the world. So I listened to what she had to say, and I made that as important to me as she is."

Raymond's face broke into a broad grin. "That's respect and love, and a very fine thing it is. But that attitude would be tough to maintain in the face of some hard-nosed, unlovable managers that I know."

"True," Marty said, leaning forward against the table and into the conversation. "But I hear where Gary's coming from regarding communication. It's about respect. Sure, with his daughter Carly, it's about love too as well. But, in everyday communications, if we can respect the other person enough to listen attentively, and then to speak to them with skill, I mean, making sure we get our points across, that's the ticket. We have to communicate: listen, then present."

"Most people don't communicate well," Terry said. "That's a given, but I do think it's worthwhile to buck a bad trend and do something positive. Let's face it, the work situations we find ourselves in demand good, effective communication. As supervisors, we need to communicate effectively. It comes with the territory. Think of the impact we could have in our different work environments, the five of us, if we made it a point to practice the kind of communication we've been talking about."

"It's sure worth a try," Raymond said.

"It is," Sylvie said, and she raised her tea-cup in a toast to trying for better communication. All of the other Supers joined her, and each of them clinked their tea-cup with the others in turn.

Inukshuk Nine - Communicate: Listen, then Present

Listen Respectfully

Adopt a Listening Mode Attitude

Use Questions as Probes

Clarify Purpose

Remove Listening Blocks

Profile Presentation Audience

Prepare Presentation Core Thought

Determine Presentation Organization Strategy

Overcome Fears and Practice

Use Communication Skills in Everyday Situations

Super Skill: Improve Work Processes

Profile Ten: Sylvie Morriseau

Sylvie Morriseau begins an in-depth review of plant processes to make improvements wherever possible. Through discussions with other Supervisors, she learns about useful approaches in making improvements to work processes through various kinds of flowcharting. Sylvie uses these approaches in working with her team.

Thursday Dim Sum

"You know my story," Sylvie began. "I've been given the job of improving processes, anywhere and everywhere in my plant. I've been pretty good at figuring things out and solving a few problems on the line as they come up. But now I'm working with different teams throughout the plant. I really don't know where to start. I'd appreciate hearing any suggestions you have."

Terry's face lit up. "I've got a few ideas for you," he said. "I've spent a lot of time looking at processes, and the overall system these processes serve. The best place to start Sylvie

149

is by thinking in terms of systems. What I mean is, you have to start with the big picture. What are you in business for? What's your purpose? For instance, let's start here, right here. Take a look around. If we think about this restaurant using systems thinking, we know that its purpose is to serve food to customers, to us. The system that delivers the food to us is made up of many, many processes and capabilities, and they're all linked, and inter-related. It's all quite amazing when you think about it. Look. We're sitting here and enjoying really fine food. We're the customers, and we are what this restaurant business is all about."

Sylvie was looking a bit puzzled. "O.K., the system here is serving food to customers. But, break it down for me. What are the processes and capabilities you mentioned? How do they fit in?"

"The processes, first of all, all contribute to the purpose of the system, namely serving food to customers. But keep in mind that there are a whole whack of processes at work behind my eating this steamed shrimp roll. Somebody had to order shrimp, and dough, and spices from different suppliers. That's a process. Somebody had to prepare and cook the shrimp roll. That's another process. And then there's the waitress who brought it to our table and served it to us. That's still another process. They're all interdependent processes that fit into the system of serving food to people. Think about all of the interactions that have to take place before I put this shrimp roll into my mouth."

Terry smiled and then stabbed the shrimp roll with a chopstick and placed it into his mouth.

"O.K.," Sylvie said, "I follow you there. What about the capabilities you mentioned? What do you mean by that?"

"Capabilities are the abilities involved in doing things. It takes a lot of skill to prepare this dumpling. I know I couldn't do it. This dumpling is an output of the system. I'm at the receiving end. Good service is another capability. Ordering supplies is another capability. It goes on and on, but you have to know what to look at."

"So," Sylvie summarized, " I start with a clear purpose and focus on the capabilities that best serve my customers. And then, knowing what my customers like, the outputs, I focus on the systems, processes, and methods that have to be in place to serve them."

"Yup," Terry said. "And keep in mind that your outputs, or in this case, the shrimp dumplings, have to be continuously monitored. What I'm saying is that in order to serve this dumpling to a customer, you have to monitor the systems that produce it. The dumplings have to be consistent, so that when I come in for lunch every other Thursday, I can rely on getting the same flawless dumpling. That means, among other things, that there are standardized processes at work behind this very dumpling that I have on my chopstick, and the one I'll be enjoying the next time. Do you get it?"

"I get it," Sylvie said. "I also have to make sure that my suppliers give me the input I need to prepare your flawless dumpling."

"That's right," Raymond interjected. "Otherwise, and this happens all the time in the restaurant business, we'll take our business down the street. You'll laugh at this but sometimes, when a chef leaves to work for another restaurant, the customers will follow him. The loyalty is to the food, not the business. That's what the customers care about."

"Well, if I owned this business, I'd make sure I knew what my customers wanted," Sylvie said.

Terry signaled to the waitress. It was obvious to Sylvie and Raymond that he wanted some additional flawless dumplings.

The table grew quiet for a few moments as they enjoyed the steaming dumplings and the fragrant jasmine tea. The waitress slowly pushed the dim sum cart before her and threaded her way between the tables, stopping momentarily to show the delicacies within each bamboo basket. Once the dim sum items had been chosen, she check-marked a slip of paper indicating a purchased dish. Against the far wall, three children stood in mute wonder beside an aquarium tank containing trout and lobsters in separate enclosures.

"So," Sylvie began, "Where do I start?"

Terry motioned with a chopstick toward the busy kitchen. Waitresses were continuously moving through the heavy, swinging doors and replenishing their dim sum carts with fresh food. "Right there," Terry said, "where the work gets done. Your key functions and key roles are in there. That's where you study the work processes and core resources. Then you streamline and organize things even better, eliminating any kind of waste that you come across. The principles behind improving processes are the same whether it's this restaurant here, or your own business."

"I hear you, but how do I communicate that to my teams?"

"It's simple. Get them involved, explain the concepts behind improving processes. Start with the purpose. People really can't give their best until they know why. You know, there are six tried and true ways for getting work done in any business. The first step is to get a fix on the flow of work. If you take the time to make a simple flowchart, little boxes that define what's done, you'll be well on your way to learning how things really operate, not how they're expected to operate. The next step is to identify who does what, who the key players are, like the chef in the kitchen here. Then, take a good, hard look at the core resources, the basics that you need to run your business. That's your equipment and supplies. After you've done that, identify your best methods, the workflow that really works, and standardize them. Make sure everyone on your team uses the same method for a particular operation, and knows why. Once you've done that you'll be in a good position to eliminate waste from your operation. The final thing is to monitor the processes, and have your team involved in feedback loops, so that your systems are humming and focused. Make sense?"

"Yeah, but do you think the same approach that works out in a restaurant will work on a plant floor?"

"I'm convinced of that. Remember, we're talking about improving processes through better supervision and management. We're not leaving quality to the end, like an afterthought. We're building it into the very processes that serve the customer. That's why we want to standardize the things that are working very well. When you think about it, we can even focus our training on the tasks that organize the work and keep it moving smoothly. All it is in the end is paying really close attention to the work flow, to what drives the business, any business."

"By paying attention, you mean observing things?"

"That, and seeing common, everyday things with new eyes. Sometimes you can literally stumble on better ways of doing things. Let me give you an example. A few months ago we received the first machine for our production line. Our engineers, people who had helped design it, left our tool-setters with elaborate, detailed specs on how it operates. They looked really impressive. These instructions were attached to the machine itself. I had a really hard time understanding the instructions, and so I asked the tool-setter who runs the machine to run me through it. Do you know what he did? He totally ignored the engineer's instructions, and pulled out a crumpled piece of paper from his back pocket. The guy had written out a set of his own pencilled instructions that gave him what he needed to know to operate the machine. In the end we used his notes to standardize operations for that machine. It became the training guide for new operators as well. The engineer's specs were too complicated and contained a lot of unnecessary information. We just wanted the need to know stuff, and we got it. But I have to tell you, we got it by accident."

"And a little observation," Sarah said.

"You got it. That's what it takes, observation, and the right attitude."

"So, is there a simple way of remembering all of this?"

"I use a few models or frameworks that help to get things started. One of the simplest is based on three questions. You can call it the three-question model if you want to get fancy. What are you trying to do or accomplish? What change can you make that will result in an improvement? How will you know when a change is an improvement? These questions aren't in any sequential order. You can start with any of them depending on your preference and the process involved."

"I guess my preference would be to start with my purpose and then go from there."

"That makes sense," Terry said. "The three question model would serve you well. It's simple and proven. It'll work with any kind of process improvement work."

"Any other models?'

"Sure. One of the most popular is plan, do, study, and act. Call it PDSA. In the planning stage you define your purpose and set about asking the kinds of questions that are related to the improvement you want. In the doing stage you follow through and determine how easy your plan is for actually making it happen. Then, during the study phase, you monitor all sorts of things, indicators and information that let you know if you're on course or not. Finally, during the 'act' stage, you focus on the adjustments and changes you've had to make to your original intervention. At this stage you can also standardize the new methods you're using. Is that clear, or am I beginning to confuse you?"

"Plan, do, study, and act. It's clear enough for now. I learn best from doing, Terry. It's going to take some time before I've got things under control."

"Good. These models or frameworks are just that. You can use either of them to structure the questions you need to ask about the process you want to improve.   All of this is built on the work of a man named W. Edwards Deming."

"I like the approach."

"It works."

Sylvie suddenly realized how quiet the others had been while she and Terry had been talking. Turning to face them she understood why. Raymond was opening a small, dark green parcel, triangular in shape while Gary was obviously enjoying some soup. Marty was intent on the delicacy before him, miniature spare ribs covered in a black sauce in a saucer-size dish. The aroma of garlic wafted in her direction. As Raymond unwrapped the sheet of lotus leaf, Sylvie saw steam rise from the savory rice inside. Terry was watching too and swallowed hard, unconsciously. Raymond laughed. 'Would you like to join us?"

"Sylvie," Terry cried out, "how could we have been so remiss in our duties?"

Raymond had ordered enough dishes for everyone, and he passed them on, in turn, to Sylvie and Terry. The waitress appeared with additional bowls of soup and set them down in the middle of the round table for ready access by everyone.

"I though everyone might want to try some *wun tong* soup with rice noodles," Raymond said.

"What is that delicious looking sauce on the spareribs?" Sylvie asked.

"That is black bean sauce with garlic."

"And is that rice in the green wrapper?"

"Ah yes, that's steamed rice with a bit of pork inside. The green wrapper is lotus leaf."

"Raymond, I just love being surprised with these treats."

Terry was already munching on one of the spareribs with one hand and giving a thumbs-up signal to Raymond with the other. Gary was using his chopsticks, a little unsteadily, to gather the thick, white rice noodles in his soup. Sylvie was watching him with undisguised interest. Once he had captured several of them, he downed them all at once, leaving a single noodle hanging precariously from his mouth. With a sharp intake of his breath, he slurped it back, winking at Sylvie as he did so. Marty applauded.

"Not bad," Marty said, "considering that I don't think you've had any formal training with chopsticks. Just look at that. I'm amazed at your dexterity- soup with chopsticks."

Gary smiled through a mouthful of noodles. He hadn't enjoyed a bowl of soup like this in a long time. He was savoring every mouthful. He noticed Terry was dipping one of the spareribs into a small saucer of chili oil. Gary decided to pour a spoonful of it over his remaining noodles. Then he scooped up a mouthful on his chopsticks and swallowed. After a moment Gary realized the full power of a well-made chili sauce.

"Whew, boy is that hot," he said. "Sylvie, could you pass the water please."

"Sure thing. There you go."

Gary's face was bright crimson. "Terry, I don't understand how you can take so much of that hot sauce. I'm suffering." He took a great gulp of the water.

Terry leaned back on his chair and laughed. "The secret is to always take very small portions. A light touch of it is enough."

Sylvie turned to Terry again, tilting her head to one side thoughtfully, and said, "I'm thinking of my team and how to get things going with them. You've given me some ideas on useful models and frameworks for improving processes. That's a good place to start from. But, do you have any suggestions on how to really get them involved?"

"Use flowcharts."

"What do you mean?"

"You need to picture any process that you want to improve or change. That's where to begin. Get your team to identify the actual flow or sequence of events in the process you're examining. Get them to do it. You need an overview of it."

"Why?"

"For a lot of reasons. Flowcharting can show you any problem areas, or unnecessary duplications, or bottlenecks. It can help you identify the causes of a problem. If the team does it together, examining a process I mean, they can come to agreement on the exact steps involved in the process. From there, they can pinpoint which activities are having impact on the performance of the process."

"So they can fix things."

"If need be. Keep in mind that it's important to map out, to flowchart, the process as it actually is. After the team has done that, they can map out the process as it should be. Then, by comparing and contrasting the actual against the ideal, you can begin to identify any changes that are needed or the improvement opportunities for the process you're looking at. Does that make any sense, or am I complicating things?"

"I'm following you, but I'm worried about the mechanics of it. How do I actually do it? How do I do the flowcharting thing?"

"Don't worry about that. It's simple if you follow a few basic rules."

"Tell me about it."

Terry took a pen from his pocket and drew three symbols, one above the other, on his napkin. Then, he showed it to Sylvie. "You use an oval to show the start of the process or the materials, resources, and inputs you need. An oval can also show the end results, or output of the process. The box here is used to show an activity or task performed in the process. This diamond shows those points in the process where a decision is required, or where a yes or no question is being asked. Is that O.K. so far?"

"It's good."

"So, you use ovals to define where the process that you're studying starts and ends. It's important to frame the boundaries of what you're looking at. Then, you get your team to brainstorm all of the inputs, activities, decisions, and outputs from the beginning of the process to the end. It's all done with these three basic symbols. Once the process has been brainstormed, you can sequence the steps involved, the order in which they're actually carried out."

"Would I use a large white board and markers to flowchart everything?"

"Sure, if you have a really large one. What I've found that works is a series of flipchart sheets taped against a wall, side by side. I always use post-it notes, the larger ones, to indicate the steps involved. The beauty of it is that you can move them around the flipchart sheets and arrange them in the right order. Oh yes, there's one other thing that goes with the symbols. You use arrows to show the direction or flow of the process."

"Do you mean like this?" Sylvie had drawn a simple flowchart on the back of her napkin using the symbols Terry had shown her. She had indicated the flow between the five symbols with arrows.

"That's it exactly," Terry said.

Raymond passed them some fresh napkins. "You may need these," he said smiling.

"I like a man who anticipates my needs Raymond," Sylvie said.

"I wouldn't touch that comment with a ten-foot pole," Marty said.

Raymond smiled. "But you see," he said, "that's exactly what we want good businesses to do. We want them to anticipate the needs of their customers."

"There's one thing I forgot to mention," Terry said. "When you're doing your flowcharting, make sure that you're consistent in the level of detail that you're showing. What I'm saying is that some flowcharts are highly detailed with all kinds of steps and sub-steps. Others just show the major actions in a process. It all depends on what you want to do, your purpose."

"What if we make a mistake somewhere along the way? Will that throw everything off?"

"After you've got your flowchart down, it's important to review it and make sure it's complete. Check with all of the people actually involved in the process. They have to validate it, and make certain that you've captured the way things actually move. You may find a mistake or two, but that's all right. In fact, that's what it's all about. You want your team to identify and then correct any mistakes that crop up."

"I'm anxious to try it out," Sylvie said, leaning forward with her elbows against the edge of the table. "I think the whole exercise will be great for the team."

"I've had a lot of success with using flowcharting, even between different departments, different functions," Terry added.

"But I thought we were just looking at a process within a department," Sylvie commented.

"You can always go further and look at processes between departments. You just have to indicate departments or responsibilities at the top, or to the side of the flowcharting details. This way everyone knows who has input on certain activities or decisions."

"I like that approach. It widens the circle."

"Once you get into it," Terry said, "there are all kinds of variations you can use, depending on what it is you're trying to do. A top-down flowchart, for instance, simply lists a horizontal band of key actions or steps in a process at the top of the chart. And then, beneath each one of those major steps, there is a vertical listing of the sub-steps involved. I've always found it elegant in a way."

"What do you mean?"

"I'm talking about the graphic representation of a process, the design of it. It's a structured, visual display of something people do. I've always thought of it as elegant."

"Elegant and useful," Raymond said.

"Yes, elegant and useful," Terry said. "They're very compatible terms."

"Boy," Gary said, "I never thought I'd hear supervisors talking about their work as being 'elegant.' You people never cease to amaze me."

"Just remember, you're one of us now," Marty said.

Terry turned back to face Sylvie. "The proof is in the pudding," he said.

"O.K., I'll try it out with my team, and see what happens."

At the Plant

When Sylvie arrived at the team meeting room thirty minutes before it was scheduled to begin, Ransom Myers was already there. He was at the white board, and he was working feverishly on a very detailed flowchart. It resembled a comprehensive electrical wiring diagram. He glanced at Sylvie, nodded in greeting, and continued his activity. He appeared to be racing to complete it.

Puzzled, Sylvie asked, "Good morning Ransom. What, may I ask, are you doing?"

Without turning to face her, Ransom answered, "I got your agenda stating that we'd be flowcharting and reviewing our product design process. Since that's one of my primary responsibilities, I thought I'd speed things up by having the flowchart up and ready by the time the team got here." He seemed to be attacking the white board with his red marker, making it shake and tremble against the wall with his forceful strokes.

"Wait a minute," Sylvie said. "My plan for the meeting today was to develop the flowchart together, with everybody's input. It's a team thing. That's why it's on the agenda I sent out to everyone. We need to do it together, as a team."

Ransom turned away from the white board and glared at her. He tossed the marker on the table, where it bounced once and then hit the floor. He didn't bother to pick it up. "Here we go again," he said, utterly exasperated. "Just when I think you're on the up and up about this team thing, you lower the boom on me. I've spent a lot of time mapping out this process. I even got the Production Manager to take a look at it yesterday to make sure everything was there. I do all this. I try to save the team a big chunk of time. I don't have to do it, but I do it. I do all this work, and you're in my face. I don't even know why I bother."

"But I didn't ask you to do this! In fact, I didn't want you to do this. This is a team thing- something we have to do together."

Visibly frustrated, Ransom plopped heavily into the closest chair. He was a big man, considerably overweight, and the chair came close to buckling under him. The rest of the team began to arrive, and they could sense the tension immediately. Everyone sat very quietly, looked intently at the flowchart on the white board, and waited. Ransom folded his arms across his chest and stared fixedly at a point in the middle of the board room table.

Sylvie took a deep breath and welcomed everyone. She reviewed the agenda and spent five minutes outlining the purpose of the meeting, specifically, to map out the product design process, "as a team," she emphasized. "We'll do it together, step by step, and then review it for accuracy."

As she spoke, Ransom stood up and erased the chart he had drawn on the white board. He was very careful not to leave a single trace of his markings on the board. When he was finished, he returned to his seat. Sylvie paused for a moment and thanked him. He gave no indication that he had heard anything. Soon, the team was busy brainstorming the steps involved in the process and everyone was contributing freely, except for Ransom.

"I just want to remind everyone," Sylvie said, "that silence will be taken to mean agreement, as we've established in our team meeting guidelines. So, let's continue."

Sylvie's team began to review and validate the flowchart. She observed that Ransom was studying the chart and appeared to be totally absorbed in the exercise. Suddenly, he cleared his throat, a little too audibly. Sylvie sprang at the opportunity to include him.

"Ransom, do you have anything to add?"

"Some of the decision points... I didn't know about them. That's not the way it's supposed to work."

Sylvie nodded. "What we're looking at here is the way things actually work. This flowchart is based on what people actually do. The next step, after validating what we've got here, is to implement any necessary changes, and later to monitor them, to see if they're working."

Ransom leaned forward in his seat. "Why not just eliminate the problems? Strike them out of the equation. It'll save us a lot of time."

"We want to get at the causes of those problems, the very roots of them," Sylvie said. " We need to identify the causes before we can make any meaningful changes. That's one of the key steps before we can standardize this process."

Ransom shifted in his seat. "You know, I see now where you're going with this. It's different from what I thought we were going to do, but I see it now," he said grudgingly. " We sure have a lot of work to do. You should have warned us, Boss."

Sylvie was beginning to understand Ransom's abrasive approach. It was not meant to be offensive, but it often came across that way.

"I don't want to be anybody's boss," she replied. " I do want to be a team member though. And I agree with you, we've just scratched the surface. We've got a long way to go."

"Let's do it," Ransom said, turning to face the white board with a huge grin.

Inukshuk Ten : Improve Work Processes

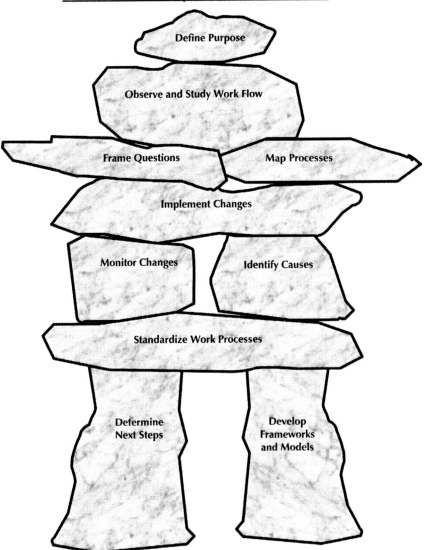

Epilogue

They left the restaurant with a feeling of full contentment, as much for the conversation as for the food. When Terry rubbed his belly with unconscious satisfaction, Raymond laughed loudly, and then said, "You're like the smiling Buddha when you rub your stomach."

"That's what I'm afraid of. I'm getting to enjoy this food too much."

"Too much of a good thing, especially dim sum, is never enough," Marty offered.

"For my waistline it is. It's an ongoing struggle for me," Terry said with a smile and a tone in his voice that implied he really didn't care all that much about it. A brilliant flash of scarlet suddenly flew across their line of vision. It startled them with its deep-red, blurring speed.

"What was that?" Gary asked.

"A cardinal, the first I've seen in a long time," Raymond said, following its flight to a stand of cedars in a park across the street. He observed the subtle, feathering movement of the cardinal's tail as it landed in perfect, natural alignment.

"Wow, it's magnificent when it's flying like that," Sylvie said, her voice tinged with delight. She remembered for a fleeting instant her favorite Aunt Marie had loved cardinals and that everyone had always given her gifts of pictures and replicas of the bird now lost in the cedars.

"A thing of beauty," Raymond said. "You'll have to pardon my analogy, but I think that flying bird is a lot like a Supervisor using a complete skill set, someone at the height of their powers, just what we've been talking about all these months. "

"Well," Sylvie said, grinning broadly, "I never heard anyone liken a Supervisor to a bird before, but the working world could sure use that kind of beauty. I'm not accustomed to thinking about supervisory skills like that, but it's exact."

They spent a few minutes saying their good-byes. They had decided not to meet for lunch over the summer. Raymond asked them to wait a moment while he went to his van and returned with a few large red folders. He handed one folder to each of them in turn.

"Inside you'll find several inukshuk drawings- one for each of the skill sets we've been discussing all these months. Remember, the skills aren't cast in concrete. Skill sets are quick and fluid like a bird in flight. Work situations are constantly changing, and you have to adapt on the fly. "

"Thanks for this," Marty said. The others nodded in agreement.

"Don't thank me," Raymond said smiling. "Thank the Inuit for the graphic concept of giving direction. And we all contributed to the identification of skills for each of the supervisory skill sets. It's all about communication, and it always has been."

"I'm gonna miss you all, over the summer. I don't know what I would have done without your guidance and input," Gary said.

"And yours," Sylvie replied. "You're a Super too, remember. We explored all of these issues together, and that's what makes it so special. It's real stuff."

"Sure is," Marty emphasized. "I've always thought that change comes about as a result of experience. We've pooled together our supervisory experiences, and what we've come up with is something tough and durable and resilient.

166

Something that will make our job easier," he said, tapping his head lightly with the red folder.

"Right on," Terry agreed. "The really interesting thing will be the ways we use what we've learned, how we act on it. What you said about change and experience is so true. You can only change when your own experience tells you it's time to change. And the one thing I've learned is that experience and behavior are patterned. What we do, how we act, is based on our habits, the patterns of our daily routines. We've got to internalize everything to really make it happen."

"Boy," Gary said, "That hot sauce really got to you. I'm not sure I follow what you've said, but you sure make it sound convincing."

Terry laughed. "Sorry, it's not the chili sauce Gary. Every now and then, something connects, and if I don't express it, I'll lose it."

"It's called an epiphany Terry," Raymond said.

"That sounds like an exotic animal," Gary said.

"It's kind of like that," Raymond said, enjoying the simile. "A cluster of ideas fires up the old brain cylinders and nothing is ever the same again. Everything changes."

"I sure hope so," Terry said. "Bye everyone. See you in September."

About The Author

Frank Buchar has worked internationally as a supervisory/ management consultant. As a business writer for newspapers and various training periodicals, he cites the crucial role of the Supervisor as being "the most strategic position in an organization despite it being a role suspended between management and employees. Supervisors are on the fault line between management and employees, pressured equally by both groups and expected to perform miracles with little incentive- usually for only a ten or fifteen per cent uplift in salary. There is not a position in any organization that is caught by so many pressures from both above and below."

Printed in the United Kingdom
by Lightning Source UK Ltd.
119088UK00001B/155